I0101975

ISBN 978-0-9817745-7-2

♻ Printed on recycled paper, using soy-based ink

Table of Contents

Figures

Tables

Introduction

When all is said and done, good irrigation management is nothing more mysterious than maintaining a suitable environment for growing crops, mainly by keeping soils from getting too wet or too dry.

There are many ways to accomplish this goal. Most irrigators should 1) check actual soil moisture levels in the field, 2) know the amount of irrigation water they are applying, 3) know general irrigation guidelines for the crops they are growing, and 4) track crop water use or evapotranspiration as the season goes by. The pages that follow describe several ways of doing each of these things.

This book focuses on conserving and protecting water, soil, energy, and other natural resources. It is not intended to be a complete irrigation textbook, and many topics are not covered. For example:

• This book is not intended to be a guide to choosing, planning, evaluating, or designing an irrigation system. The discussion generally assumes that an irrigation system is already in place.

• There is little discussion of diversion structures, efficient storage of water in reservoirs, or efficient conveyance of water to the farm in pipelines or ditches. It is generally assumed that irrigation water is available at the field.

• Only a handful of crops are described in detail: a representative sampling of commonly irrigated crops along with a few that pose special management challenges.

No one knows more than you do about your fields, crops, and irrigation system. No guidebook can substitute for the powers of judgment, observation, and local knowledge that good irrigators acquire over time. So adjust, adapt, or reject any suggestion in this book if it doesn't fit your situation or doesn't seem to be

1

working. Use every kind of information you can find about how your soils and crops are responding, proceed cautiously, and test every recommendation with direct observations in the field.

The exclamation mark ! indicates safety hazards, potential equipment damage, possible harm to crops, or other situations calling for extra caution.

Know Your Soils

This chapter explains

• how soils are classified

• how soils hold water

• soil moisture terminology

Soil Textures & Types

The water-holding capacity of a soil depends on its soil type, organic matter content, and past management practices, among other things.

Soils are classified into one of about a dozen standard *textures* or *texture classes,* based on the proportion of sand, silt, and clay particles. Sand particles are larger than clay particles, with silt particles falling in between. For example, a soil that is 20 percent clay, 60 percent silt, and 20 percent sand (by weight) would be classified as silt loam. Other texture classes are sand, loamy sand, sandy loam, loam, silt, sandy clay loam, clay loam, silty clay loam, sandy clay, silty clay, and clay.

Coarse-textured soils have a high percentage of sand and *fine-textured* soils have a high percentage of clay. Fine-textured soils generally hold more water than coarse-textured soils, although some medium-textured soils hold as much or more *plant-available* water than some clay soils.

Soils are also given names and classified into *soil types* or *soil series,* based mainly on soil-building factors such as geology, chemistry, age, and location. There are over 20,000 named soils in the U.S. alone, with names often referring to a town or landmark near where the soil was first recognized. For example, the Houston Black series is a clay soil formed under prairie vegetation in Texas. The Myakka series is a wet sandy soil found in Florida. The full description of a soil series includes a number of layers or horizons, starting at the surface and moving downward.

To identify the soil types or series in your fields, refer to a soil survey. Soil surveys may be available from your local NRCS or Extension office, from sources on the internet, or from your local *conservation district*.

❗ Caution: The information on these soil surveys or maps is somewhat generic, and you'll almost certainly want help interpreting and adapting the information for local conditions.

How Soils Hold Water

As water infiltrates soil, pore spaces between the soil particles fill with water. When the pores are completely saturated by a heavy rain or irrigation, some of the water — *gravitational water* — percolates down and below the root zone. (Gravitational water may drain for a few hours in sandy soils, or days or even weeks in clay soils.) Evaporation at the soil surface pulls water upward through capillary forces, while capillary forces also hold water around the soil particles. When a balance is reached between gravitational and capillary forces (a condition known as *field capacity*), water stops moving downward and is held by surface tension in the soil. This *capillary water* stored in the root zone is the most important water for crop production.

The water-holding force of soil, or *soil water tension,* is affected by soil type as well as by the amount of water in the soil. For example, clay soils have small pores and hold water more tightly than silt soils, with their larger pores. Not all capillary water is available for plants to use. As soil water is depleted, the films of water remaining around the soil particles become thinner, until they are eventually held in the soil with more tension than plants can overcome.

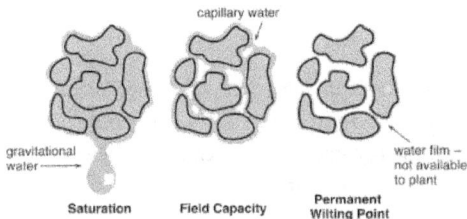

Figure 1. Saturation, Field Capacity, and Permanent Wilting Point

When plants can no longer extract sufficient water from the soil, they begin to wilt. Some plant species can extract more water than others. Young plants, or those with limited or superficial root systems, can generally extract less water than older or thicker-rooted plants.

Definitions: Soil Moisture & Crop Water-Use

The following terms will be useful in explaining the main purpose of irrigation management: keeping soils from becoming too wet or too dry.

Soil moisture terminology and definitions vary widely, although these variations usually make little or no practical difference to irrigators.

Saturation — The soil moisture condition where pore spaces between soil particles are completely filled with water. Water added to saturated soil will drain downward or run off the surface. Saturated soil is too wet for good plant growth, making little or no oxygen available to the roots.

Field Capacity (sometimes called *soil water storage* capacity) — The soil moisture condition where gravitational water has drained out and only capillary water remains. Field capacity should be viewed as the upper (wet) limit of good irrigation management. As soils become wetter than

5

field capacity, roots start taking in far less water, oxygen is depleted, and plant growth decreases.

Crop Stress Point (sometimes called the *minimum balance*) — The soil moisture condition where plants can no longer extract enough water to meet their requirements and begin to experience serious damage to their growth and development. At or beyond the crop stress point, soils are too dry for good crop growth.

Permanent Wilting Point — The soil moisture condition where agricultural plants can no longer extract the tightly held films of capillary water from the soil at a rate fast enough to recover from wilting. The permanent wilting point should not be confused with *temporary wilting*, the normal cycle of plant wilting during the day followed by recovery at night.

Soil Water Tension (sometimes called soil-water *potential*) — The force holding water to soil particles or, conversely, the work required for plants to transport water through soil. Soil water tension is usually measured in *centibars* (cb). The larger the centibar number, the harder the plant must work and the drier the soil. Sometimes centibar measurements are expressed in negative numbers.

Available Water Capacity (AWC) (sometimes called *plant-available water* or simply *available water*) — The amount of water that a soil can make available to plants; the difference between the amount of water stored at field capacity and the amount of water stored at the permanent wilting point. AWC is usually expressed in inches of water per foot or per inch of soil depth. For example, some clay loam soils hold 2.2 inches of available water per foot of soil depth. A three-foot deep layer of this soil would hold 6.6 inches of available water. Note that, in this definition, AWC varies by soil texture and type but does not vary by crop.

Root Zone (or *rooting depth*) — *Potential rooting depth* is
the deepest unrestricted rooting depth attainable by a crop.
Because of physical and chemical barriers in the soil, the
actual maximum rooting depth may be less than the potential
rooting depth.

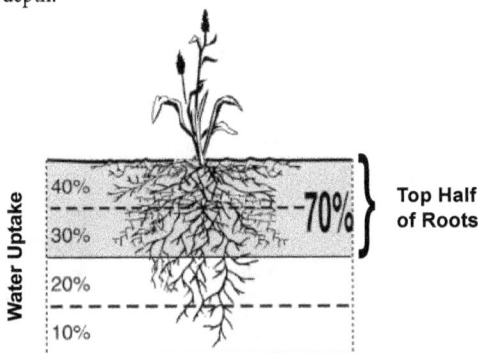

Figure 2. Effective Root Zone: the top half of the actual
rooting depth, which supplies about 70% of the crop's water needs.

Effective Root Zone — The upper portion of the root zone,
where plants get most of their water — generally considered
to be the upper half of the actual maximum rooting depth,
where about 70 percent of the plant's water is taken up.

Management Allowable Depletion (MAD) (sometimes
called *allowable depletion, maximum allowed depletion,
allowable soil water depletion, management allowable deficit,*
etc.) — The percentage of available water that can safely
be depleted without seriously affecting plant growth and
development. For many crop types and growth stages, MAD is
in the range of 40 to 60 percent of AWC. In general, irrigation
management should be based on MAD in the effective root
zone.

7

Allowable Depletion Balance (sometimes called *remaining usable water*) — The difference between the amount of water currently stored in soils, at a given time, and the amount stored at the crop stress point. The allowable depletion balance should be viewed as the irrigator's safety cushion. Once this amount reaches zero, plants will begin to experience serious damage to their growth and development.

Evapotranspiration (ET) (sometimes called *crop water use*) — The movement or loss of water from the soil to the atmosphere, through the combined effects of evaporation from the soil surface and transpiration by plants. ET is usually measured in inches per day. Note that ET does not include evaporation from wet plant leaves or evaporation of spray between a sprinkler and the ground.

Intake Rate (sometimes called *infiltration rate*) — The rate at which the soil can accept water, usually expressed in inches of water per hour. If the application rate exceeds the intake rate, ponding or runoff will occur.

Summarizing much of the terminology above, soils normally dry out through a series of stages: from *saturation* to *field capacity* to the *crop stress point* to the *permanent wilting point*. Good irrigation management basically keeps soil moisture levels between field capacity and the crop stress point. At field capacity, *AWC* is the portion of water available to plants and *MAD* is the percentage of AWC that can be removed without causing serious stress. At any given time, the *allowable depletion balance* is the amount of water remaining before plants begin to experience serious stress.

Know Your Soil Moisture

This chapter explains

• several ways to monitor soil moisture

• a few ways to determine the water-holding capacity of your soils

• several ways to increase the water-holding capacity of your soils

Soil Moisture Monitoring

In deciding when and how much to irrigate (a process called *irrigation scheduling*), all irrigators should do some kind of soil moisture monitoring.

What Method is Right for You?

If you haven't looked into soil moisture monitoring in awhile, you may be pleasantly surprised at how inexpensive it has become to install a state-of-the-art monitoring system. In deciding among the many tools on the market:

1. Don't get too hung up on accuracy or precision. Devices will give slightly different readings, but all will track moisture trends similarly. So choose a method that you like, take the exact readings with a grain of salt, and pay more attention to the trends and changes you are seeing over time.

2. Consider your soils and crops. Some devices work better in coarse soils than fine soils, some devices work better with annual crops than with perennial crops, and so on. High-value crops may justify a more expensive monitoring system.

3. Consider the limitations imposed by your irrigation system. If you don't have much control over application rates and amounts, then precise monitoring isn't necessary or helpful.

4. Consider what's convenient for you. Some devices are portable while others are hard-wired in place. Some devices give you "raw" data while others do the calculations for you, or display readings in a graph. Some devices require cables that may interfere with tillage.

9

5. Be realistic in your expectations. Soil moisture measurement, even with the advent of ever-more-accurate devices, doesn't eliminate all guesswork or substitute for the powers of judgment and observation that good irrigators acquire over time.

The methods below are arranged roughly in order of cost, from least expensive to more expensive. All work just fine if they are used properly and diligently.

Direct Inspection

The least expensive methods rely on digging up soil samples in the field and then inspecting and feeling them.

Feel and Appearance Method

With practice and diligence, the feel and appearance method can be accurate enough for most irrigation management decisions. A soil probe, auger, core sampler, or even a hand posthole digger is superior to a shovel, since you need to retrieve samples from the entire root zone.

Take walnut-sized soil samples from various locations and depths in the field, appropriate to your crop's root zone. Then use Table 1, page 12, to estimate the soil water content of your samples.

Hand-Push Probe

You can use a hand-push probe to determine the depth of wetted soil, as well as to retrieve soil samples. These extremely handy probes cost under $100, and are one of the fastest and easiest ways to check moisture anywhere in your fields.

Push the probe vigorously into the soil by putting your weight on the handle without turning. The probe will stop abruptly when it reaches dry soil. (Rocks and gravel also stop the probe, but these

Figure 3. Obtaining soil sample with a hand-push probe

are easily detected by a metallic click.) Check the mark on the shaft to determine the depth of the wetted soil. To obtain a soil sample, twist the probe after pushing it into the ground. It will be full of soil when you pull it up.

Meters & Sensors

More sophisticated devices measure some physical property of the soil that is correlated with soil moisture. Some portable sensing tools are pushed directly down into the soil or into an access tube implanted in the soil. Other systems rely on buried sensors that are either hard-wired to a fixed meter, or else have long attached electrodes that are left above-ground and hooked to a portable meter.

Soil Moisture Blocks

Electrical resistance blocks work on the principle that water conducts electricity. The wetter the soil, the lower the electrical resistance and the better the block conducts electricity. The two most common types of electrical resistance blocks are *gypsum blocks* (with a short life of as little as only one year but a low cost of $5 to $15 apiece) and *granular matrix sensors* (lasting three to seven years or more and costing $30 to $45 each.) Freezing can cause cracking and premature aging in gypsum blocks, but will generally not hurt granular matrix sensors.

Electrical resistance blocks work by absorbing water from the surrounding soil. They need to be buried carefully, with good soil contact and no air pockets—something that may be difficult to achieve in coarse or gravelly soils. When burying any soil moisture sensing device, your goal is to install each sensor in surroundings that are representative of the field. So be careful to minimize soil compaction and disturbance to the surrounding canopy cover. Avoid killing nearby plants by stepping on them.

Electrical resistance blocks may be read either with a data logger (next section) or with a portable hand-held meter. These meters, costing $150 to $600, generally either show

(Continued on page 15)

12

Table 1. Determining Soil Water Content by Feel and Appearance

	Soil Texture				% of Available Water Capacity (AWC)
	Coarse*	Moderately Coarse*	Medium*	Moderately Fine and Fine*	
	Free water appears when soil is bounced in hand.	Free water is released with kneading.	Free water can be squeezed out.	Puddles and free water forms on surface.	Exceeds field capacity – runoff & deep percolation.
	Upon squeezing, no free water appears on soil, but wet outline of ball is left on hand.				100% – At field capacity
	Tends to stick together, forms a weak crumbly ball under pressure.	Forms weak ball that breaks easily; does not stick.	Forms a ball and is very pliable; sticks readily if relatively high in clay.	Ribbons out between thumb and finger; has a slick feeling.	70 – 80% of AWC
	Tends to stick together. May form a very weak ball under pressure.	Tends to ball under pressure, but seldom holds together.	Forms a ball, somewhat plastic; sticks slightly under pressure.	Forms a ball; ribbons out between thumb and finger.	50 – 70% of AWC
For most crops, irrigation should begin at 40 to 60% of AWC.					
	Appears to be dry; does not form a ball under pressure.	Appears to be dry; does not form a ball under pressure.	Somewhat crumbly but holds together under pressure.	Somewhat pliable; balls up under pressure.	25 – 50% of AWC
	Dry, loose, single-grained flow through fingers.	Dry, loose, flows through fingers.	Powdery dry, sometimes slightly crusted but easily breaks down into powder.	Hard, baked, cracked; sometimes has loose crumbs on surface.	0 – 25% of AWC

Adapted from *NRCS Irrigation Guide*, USDA Natural Resources Conservation Service, 1997.
*For an explanation of these soil textures, see Table 2 on facing page.

Table 2. Typical Intake Rates by Soil Texture and Irrigation Method (Inches per Hour)

Soil Texture	Sprinkler	Furrow	Border & Basin
Very coarse texture—very coarse sands (1.0 to 2.0 mm)	1.0+	4.0+	4.0+
Coarse texture—coarse sands, fine sands, and loamy sands (0.50 to 1.0 mm)	0.4–1.5	0.6–3.0	2.0–4.0
Moderately coarse texture—sandy loams and fine sandy loams (0.25 to 0.50 mm)	0.3–1.25	0.4–1.9	1.0–4.0
Medium texture—loams, silt loams, and silt (0.25 to 0.50 mm)	0.5–0.7	0.3–1.2	0.5–1.5
Moderately fine texture—sandy clay loams, clay loams, and silty clay loams (0.01 to 0.05 mm)	0.1–0.5	0.2–1.0	0.3–1.0
Fine texture—sandy clays, silty clays, and clays (less than 0.01 mm)	0.1–0.2	0.1–0.5	0.1–0.3

Adapted from NRCS *Irrigation Guide*, USDA Natural Resources Conservation Service, 1997.

❘ **Caution: Values vary widely within each texture class. A soil survey will provide**
● **more accurate values.**

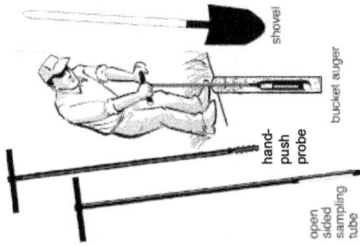

Figure 4. Soil Sampling Tools

shovel

bucket auger

hand-push probe

open sided sampling tube

Figure 5. Determining Soil Texture by the "Feel Method"

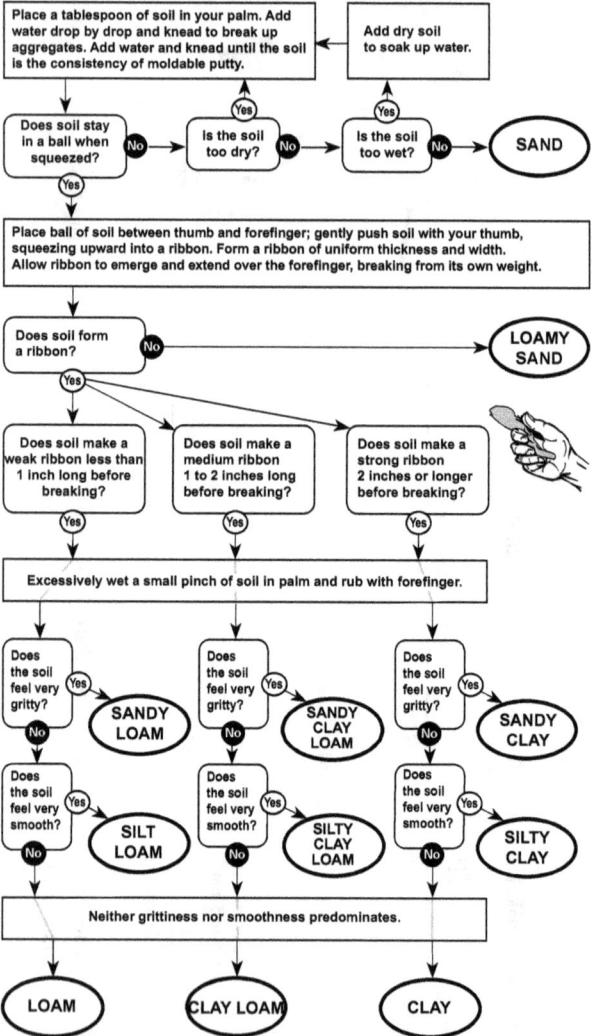

Place a tablespoon of soil in your palm. Add water drop by drop and knead to break up aggregates. Add water and knead until the soil is the consistency of moldable putty.

← Add dry soil to soak up water.

Does soil stay in a ball when squeezed? — No → Is the soil too dry? — No → Is the soil too wet? — No → **SAND**

(Yes → Add dry soil to soak up water)

Yes ↓

Place ball of soil between thumb and forefinger; gently push soil with your thumb, squeezing upward into a ribbon. Form a ribbon of uniform thickness and width. Allow ribbon to emerge and extend over the forefinger, breaking from its own weight.

Does soil form a ribbon? — No → **LOAMY SAND**

Yes ↓

Does soil make a weak ribbon less than 1 inch long before breaking? — Yes

Does soil make a medium ribbon 1 to 2 inches long before breaking? — Yes

Does soil make a strong ribbon 2 inches or longer before breaking? — Yes

Excessively wet a small pinch of soil in palm and rub with forefinger.

Does the soil feel very gritty? — Yes → **SANDY LOAM**
No ↓
Does the soil feel very smooth? — Yes → **SILT LOAM**
No ↓

Does the soil feel very gritty? — Yes → **SANDY CLAY LOAM**
No ↓
Does the soil feel very smooth? — Yes → **SILTY CLAY LOAM**
No ↓

Does the soil feel very gritty? — Yes → **SANDY CLAY**
No ↓
Does the soil feel very smooth? — Yes → **SILTY CLAY**
No ↓

Neither grittiness nor smoothness predominates.

LOAM   **CLAY LOAM**   **CLAY**

Adapted from *NRCS Irrigation Guide*, USDA Natural Resources Conservation Service, 1997.

14

SOIL MOISTURE

NCAT photo

Figure 6. Granular matrix sensor.

the electrical resistance reading from the sensor in ohms
or else convert resistance to centibars. You can check more
locations with a hand-held meter, and possibly save money
compared to the cost of a data logger. But a data logger will take
measurements far more often, giving you a better understanding
of the soil-water environment.

Data Loggers

Soil moisture data loggers are typically battery-operated devices, hard-wired to buried electrical resistance block sensors. At
regular intervals, the data logger sends a current through each
sensor, measuring electrical conductance. The measurements
are converted into soil moisture readings and stored in memory.
Data loggers with a graphical display show several days or weeks
worth of readings in a bar graph, allowing you to see recent soil
moisture trends at a glance, on the screen. Depending on their
features, soil moisture data loggers may cost from $60 to $500,
not including sensors or cable.

A major advantage of data loggers is that, no matter how busy
you get, the monitor automatically checks and records your soil
moisture. You can store a season's worth of data for viewing at a
more convenient time. A disadvantage is that a limited number
of sensors (typically 6 to 15) can be connected to the monitor.
Installation generally also requires running cable from the data
logger to each sensor.

15

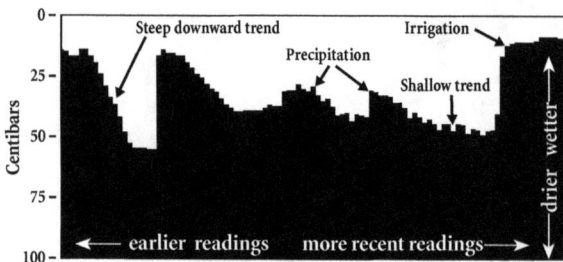

Figure 7. Data Logger Graphical Display, Showing 5 Weeks of Readings

A common indicator of soil moisture is soil water tension

Some soil moisture monitoring tools give *volumetric* readings — inches per foot or per inch of soil — while others indicate the level of *soil water tension*. Soil water tension is usually measured in *centibars* (cb), where a centibar is 1/100th of a *bar*, and a bar is roughly equivalent to one atmosphere of pressure. Centibars measure the force that a plant must exert to extract water from the soil. As the plant works harder to remove water, the centibar number increases. So larger centibar numbers mean drier soil.

Soil water tension levels mean different things in different soils and so — unfortunately — there's no simple way to translate centibar readings into water volumes or vice versa. Depending on soil texture, for example, field capacity may be between about 10 and 33 cb. Coarse soils (such as sands and sandy clay loams) have released 50 percent of their available water by the time soils have dried out to 40-50 cb. On the other hand, many clay and silty soils still retain over 50 percent of available water at 80 cb.

Tensiometers

A tensiometer is an airtight water-filled tube with a porous ceramic tip on one end and a vacuum gauge on the end that extends above the ground. Tensiometers measure soil water tension, and display the reading on the vacuum gauge in centibars (cb). These devices work best in the range of 0 to 80 cb, making them better suited for coarse soils.

Tensiometers are easy to use but must be serviced regularly by filling with water and using a pump to remove air. Depending on length — from six to 48 inches — they cost $45 to $80. Because they are easy to install and remove, tensiometers are well-suited to cultivated fields and annual crops where buried blocks or cable would be awkward. They are also often used in orchards.

SOIL MOISTURE

Table 3. Irrigation Guidelines Based on Centibar Readings

Reading	Interpretation
0-10 cb	Saturated soil
10-20 cb	Most soils are at field capacity
30-40 cb	Typical range of irrigation in many coarse soils
40-60 cb	Typical range of irrigation in many medium soils
70-90 cb	Typical range of irrigation in heavy clay soils
> 100 cb	Crop water stress in most soils

Adapted from *Watermark Soil Moisture Sensors,* The Irrometer Company, Riverside, CA.

Other Tools & Techniques

Until recently, the tools below were best suited to high-value crops and scientific research. In some cases, though, high-tech features are becoming available at affordable prices.

Time domain reflectometers (from about $500 to $4,500) send an electromagnetic wave along two parallel rods inserted in the soil. This is one way of measuring the "dielectric constant" of soil, which is strongly affected by soil moisture.

Where is my soil-full point (field capacity)?
Where is my crop stress point?

Regardless of what kind of soil moisture measuring tool you are using, you can easily determine field capacity and crop stress points for your soil. To find field capacity, take a measurement when you are sure the soil profile is full of water, such as early in the spring or after a heavy rain or irrigation set. To find the crop stress point, take a measurement at the earliest signs of crop water stress. Avoid letting your soils dry out to this point in the future.

Capacitance probes ($100 to thousands of dollars)measure the dielectric constant of soil by measuring capacitance. They are becoming common in many parts of the country.

Frequency domain reflectometers ($475 to thousands of dollars) measure the dielectric constant of soil by measuring the frequency change of electromagnetic waves pulsed through the soil from a pair of electrodes.

Neutron probes are highly accurate, often used by crop consultants. They are expensive ($3,500 to $4,500) and require special training and licensing, because of the radiation safety hazard.

Infrared thermometry is based on the principle that leaf temperature is related to a plant's transpiration rate. Infrared satellite imagery to detect crop stress is under research.

Remote sensing systems use buried sensors wired to a nearby transmitter that radios sensor readings to a receiver, typically a data logger connected to a computer. These systems allow several fields to be monitored at once from a single computer.

Tips on Placing Moisture Sensors

• It's rarely practical to monitor every part of the field, so install sensors in average soil and slope areas. Avoid field edges and unusually wet or dry spots. Be careful not to trample plants at the sensor site, so that canopy cover remains typical.

- Another approach is to install sensors in part of the field with the lowest water-holding capacity (i.e. the sandiest). If you avoid water stress in this part of the field, the rest of the field should have enough water too. Be careful not to overwater, though, especially if you have wide variations in your soils.

- The question of how deeply to maintain soil moisture is a management decision, depending on crop and growth stage, soil conditions, and other factors. In general, management should focus on the effective root zone, i.e. the upper half, where plants take up most of their water.

- For effective root zones less than two feet deep, place sensors at two different depths.

- For deeper-rooted crops, you may want to place sensors at one-foot depth increments in the rooted volume. Another common strategy is to place one sensor in the top one-third and another in the bottom one-third of the root volume, as "on-off" indicators. Start irrigating when the shallow sensor begins to get dry. Stop irrigating when the deep sensor begins to get wet.

- Place a sensor below the root zone for shallow-rooted crops (including grasses), or in the lower quarter of the root zone for deeper-rooted crops, as a way of detecting deep percolation and overwatering.

- For young trees and vines, place sensors close to the plant, among the active roots. For mature trees, place sensors well away from the trunk but inside the drip line (canopy diameter).

! **Sensors may have to be relocated in orchard and vine crops as the crop and its root system develop from seedlings to mature trees and vines.**

- For drip irrigation, the ideal sensor placement is at the edge of the wetted soil volume. A sensor placed too close to an emitter will show continuously wet soil, and a sensor placed too far from an emitter will show continuously dry soil.

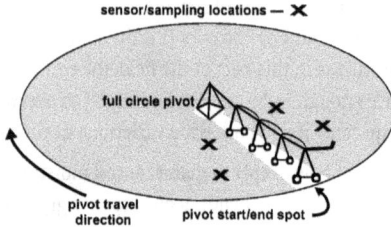

Figure 8. Soil Monitoring Sites under Pivot

• For center pivots, monitor a few sprinkler diameters from where you normally start the pivot, in the direction of pivot movement. Also monitor a few sprinkler diameters before the spot where you normally stop the pivot.

• Avoid the inner part of a pivot circle (inside the first tower), which tends to be wetter than the rest of the circle.

Changes in soil texture act as a temporary barrier to water movement

Fine soil overlying a coarse soil, or vice versa, must become very wet before water will move down through the subsoil. Under these conditions, the overlying soil holds up to three times as much water as it would in more uniform soils. If you have distinct layers of soil, you may want to monitor soil moisture in each layer separately.

Figure 9. Water Movement in Stratified Soils (Adapted from *NRCS Irrigation Guide,* USDA Natural Resources Conservation Service, 1997).

Determining the Water-Holding Capacity of Your Soils

By monitoring soil moisture, some irrigators manage to irrigate quite efficiently without knowing much about how and why their crops are using water. In many situations, though, it's very handy—or even essential—to know the available water capacity in the depth of soil that you are managing.

Using a Soil Survey

Your local NRCS or Extension office can assist you in using a soil survey to calculate the available water capacity in the depth of soil that you are managing. While the calculation itself is not difficult, the necessary information is not always easy to find, and you'll need help adapting the generic information on the soil map for your local conditions. Available water can vary within the same soil type, from year to year, and even with the season. Conditions such as rocks, compaction, hardpan, salt, organic matter content, crusting, and cracking can all dramatically affect the way your soils hold water.

Ask an NRCS or Extension employee to look up your soil information and talk to you about it. This conversation should include the entire soil profile and not just the top five feet or so that is most important for irrigation management. Local geology often has an important influence on water quality, so be alert to factors that may be at work in your subsoils.

Here's the basic process for using a soil map to calculate the available water capacity in your effective root zone: First, look up the soil series names in your fields on a soil map. Second, look in the descriptive text of the soil map to determine the texture and depth of each soil layer for that series, along with the available water capacity (AWC—sometimes called plant-available water) for each of your soil layers. While you're at it, record the intake rate for each layer, in inches per hour. Third, determine the effective root depth for your crop, using pub-

lished averages or (better) soil sampling. Finally, calculate the
total AWC for all the texture layers, to at least the effective root
depth of the mature crop grown on that field. To do this, simply
multiply the thickness of the layer times its AWC per inch or per
foot to get AWC for that layer. Then add together the AWC values
for all layers in the effective root zone to calculate total AWC.

In the example below, with soil moisture at field capacity, the
alfalfa field with Bozeman soils should hold 10.72 inches of
available water (AWC) in the five-foot effective root zone.

**! Caution: This kind of calculation should be treated
cautiously and as an approximation. Local soil conditions
often vary from published averages.**

Example:

Field No. __2__   Crop Grown __Alfalfa__

Effective Root Depth of Alfalfa at maturity____4-5 feet____

Soil Series	Soil Texture	Texture Depth	Layer Thickness	AWC (inches of water per in.)			Total AWC
Bozeman	Silt loam	0-8 in.	8 in.	×	0.17 in./in.	=	1.36 in.
	Silty clay loam	8-28 in.	20 in.	×	0.18 in./in.	=	3.6 in.
	Silt loam, silty clay loam	28-60 in.	32 in.	×	0.18 in./in.	=	5.76 in.
	Effective Root Depth:	**60 in. (5 ft.)**		**TOTAL**		**=**	**10.72 in.**

How Accurate Is Your Soil Survey?

The AWC values in a soil survey are approximations based on ideal or average characteristics for each soil series. You may be able to improve on these estimates by examining the soils in your fields.

While digging holes or looking at soil cores, note changes in soil color or texture, as well as actual root depth and other factors that influence crop growth, such as a high water table, hardpans, densely compacted restrictive layers, mineral or gravel layers, and tilth. If you encounter a compacted layer, dig up mature plant roots and see if they grow horizontally when they encounter the pan or if they are able to grow through the pan.

Pay special attention to topsoil depth. Past management practices may have reduced the depth of the *A horizon,* the top layer of soil and the one containing the most organic material. The A horizon is usually darker or browner than the layer below it. If the actual depth of this layer is different from that listed in the soil survey, adjust your calculations accordingly.

Management Practices to Increase Soil Water-Holding Capacity

You can enhance the ability of your soils to absorb and hold water by:

• Maintaining crop residue or mulch on the soil surface.
• Regularly planting and incorporating cover crops into the soil.
• Returning crop residues and applying manure to fields.
• Minimizing tillage and leaving a rough soil surface.
• Minimizing field traffic when soils are wet.
• Minimizing practices that change the soil profile.

Keeping a residue cover over the soil surface protects against surface crust formation caused by the pounding impact of rain or sprinkler irrigation water. Porous residues absorb water on impact, increasing infiltration and reducing the potential for runoff or erosion. Residues also keep the soil cool, reducing evaporation and (as a consequence) helping prevent salts from building up in the surface soil.

Adding cover crops, crop residues, or manure to the soil helps build up organic matter. For each percentage increase in organic matter, the water holding capacity of soil increases by about 50 percent. These residues also provide food and energy for organisms that form soil aggregates. Soil aggregates permit good water infiltration and reduce restrictions, encouraging healthy root growth and good access to water and nutrients.

Finding Your Actual Effective Root Zone

The effective root zone, the depth in which crops get about 70 percent of their water, varies widely depending on crop, climate, and soils, and changes throughout a plant's life. Two common ways to find your effective root zone are by excavation and by studying soil moisture extraction patterns.

In the excavation method you carefully dig plant roots from the soil, then clean, dry, and weigh them. For practical purposes, the soil depth containing 90 percent (by weight) of the roots can be considered the effective root zone.

In the soil moisture extraction method, you do periodic soil sampling, using devices such as granular matrix blocks or tensiometers. For practical purposes, the soil depth where 70 percent of total water intake takes place can be considered the effective root zone.

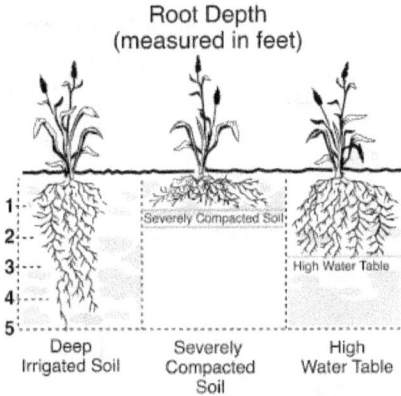

Figure 10. Restricted Root Depth

Compacted surface soils don't absorb water effectively, promoting runoff. Compacted layers also prevent water from moving freely through the soil profile, reducing water-holding capacity. You can protect against compaction by minimizing soil tillage, thus increasing the amount of residue left on the soil surface, and by avoiding wheel traffic or harvesting activities on wet soils.

Tillage that creates a rough soil surface, including clods, can help absorb water. The surface roughness blocks water flow and provides small depressions for collecting and absorbing runoff water. In addition, specialized tillage equipment can be used to create reservoirs, basins, or small pits throughout the field for collecting and absorbing water.

Land modification practices such as land-leveling or terracing often modify the soil profile, moving topsoil from high portions of the field to lower areas. As a result, the formerly high areas now have exposed subsoil, which is usually less fertile and holds less water than the original topsoil.

Table 4. Soil Texture and Typical Available Water Capacity (AWC)

Soil Texture	Typical AWC (inches per foot of depth)
Coarse Sand	0.2 - 0.8
Fine Sand	0.7 - 1.0
Loamy Sand	0.8 - 1.3
Sandy Loam	1.1 - 1.6
Fine Sandy Loam	1.2 - 2.0
Silt Loam	1.8 - 2.8
Silty Clay Loam	1.6 - 1.9
Silty Clay	1.5 - 2.0
Clay	1.3 - 1.8
Peat Mucks	1.9 - 2.9

! Caution: Values vary widely within each texture class. A soil survey will provide more accurate values. See page 6 for an explanation of the term "available water capacity."

Know How Much Water You Are Applying

This chapter explains

• how to find net water application per set for any irrigation system

• several ways to measure flows

Finding Net Water Application per Set

Some sprinkler systems and most surface irrigation systems apply water in one location for a period of time before being turned off or moved to another area of the field. This period is often called a *set* or *set time*. Other sprinkler systems, such as linear move systems and center pivots, move more or less continuously. Their set time is considered to be the period needed to cover the entire irrigated area.

Good irrigation management generally requires knowing how much water your irrigation system puts on during a given set time, then adjusting the duration or frequency of your sets so that you are putting back into the soil the amount of water that plants have used up — without watering too much or too soon.

Finding System Efficiency

In any irrigation system, some of the water that is applied is lost or fails (for a variety of reasons) to become available to the plant roots. Water is lost to deep percolation, wind drift, runoff, and evaporation during application. The term *net water application* describes the amount of water (in inches of depth) that your irrigation system actually delivers to the crop root zone during a set. To calculate net water application, you start with the gross amount of water applied and multiply it times a *system efficiency*.

Gross water applied × system efficiency = net water applied

Table 5. Attainable Irrigation System Application Efficiencies

System Type	Efficiency (%)
Surface Systems	
Level border	60-80
Furrow	60-80
Surge	65-80
Graded border	55-75
Corrugate	40-55
Wild Flood	25-40
Sprinkler Systems	
Linear move	75-90
Center pivot (low pressure)	75-90
Fixed solid set	70-85
Center pivot (high pressure)	65-80
Hand move or side roll laterals	60-75
Traveling gun	60-70
Stationary gun	50-60
Microirrigation systems	
Surface/subsurface drip	85-95
Micro spray or mist	85-90

FLOWS

Table 5 gives approximate system efficiencies for some irrigation systems: the percentage of water that actually enters and remains in the root zone.

These are only average values, for well-managed and maintained systems. Soil texture will heavily influence how your system's efficiency compares to the ranges above. In situations where true application efficiency is hard to estimate, measured *distribution uniformity (DU)* may be the most accurate "system efficiency" value to use in the formulas and calculations below. DU measures how uniformly water is infiltrating into the soil in various parts of your field. Consult your local NRCS office or conservation district for help measuring your DU.

A Shortcut Method for Most Sprinkler Systems

To estimate net water application in inches per set for most sprinkler systems (but not pivots), you can simply use the following

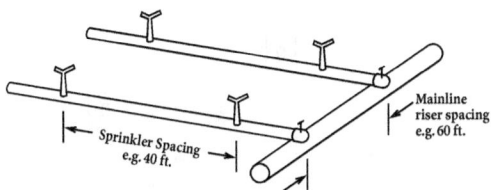

Figure 11. Spacings on Hand Move Sprinklers

two tables. Use Table 6, below, to convert nozzle size and pressure to gpm. Once you've determined your flow rate, use Table 7, on the following page, along with the correct spacing for your system, to find your system's gross water application in inches per hour. Then multiply this number times your system efficiency and times your set duration to find net water application.

Example:

A wheel line with new 9/64″ nozzles and 40 psi operating pressure, 40 foot × 40 foot sprinkler spacing (see Figure 11), 11 hour set, 65% system efficiency

From Table 6, find the 9/64″ nozzle on the left and read across to the number under 40 psi. The number is 3.7 gpm.

Then using Table 7, find the 40 × 40 spacing on the left and read across to the 3 gpm and 4 gpm columns. Since 3.7 gpm is a little more than halfway between them, estimate the gross water

Table 6. Nozzle discharge (gpm)

Nozzle Size (inch)	Nozzle Pressure, psi				
	30	40	50	60	70
3/32	1.4	1.7	1.9	2.0	2.1
1.8	2.6	3.0	3.3	3.5	3.8
9/64	3.3	3.7	4.2	4.5	4.9
5/32	3.9	4.5	5.0	5.4	5.8
11/64	4.7	5.4	6.0	6.6	7.1
3/16	5.5	6.3	7.0	7.7	8.3
13/64	6.4	7.4	8.2	9.0	9.7
7/32	7.4	8.6	9.6	10.5	11.3

Table 7. Water Application — Inches per Hour

Sprinkler Spacing	gpm/Sprinkler														
	2	3	4	5	6	7	8	9	10	11	12	15	18	20	25
30 × 30	0.21	0.32	0.43												
30 × 50			0.25	0.32	0.38	0.44	0.51	0.57	0.64	0.70	0.76				
40 × 40		0.18	0.24	0.30	0.36	0.42	0.48	0.54							
40 × 60				0.20	0.24	0.28	0.32	0.36	0.40	0.44	0.48	0.60	0.72	0.80	
50 × 60					0.19	0.22	0.26	0.29	0.32	0.35	0.39	0.48	0.58	0.64	
60 × 60							0.21	0.24	0.27	0.29	0.32	0.40	0.48	0.53	0.67
60 × 80									0.20	0.22	0.24	0.30	0.36	0.40	0.50

application at 0.22 inches per hour. Multiply 0.22 by 11 hours, the set duration, and by 0.65, the percent system efficiency.

Net water application = $0.22 \times 11 \times 0.65 = 1.6$

The net water application is 1.6 inches per set.

❗Caution: The values in the Table 6 are based on new nozzles. Flow from worn nozzles can vary significantly from these values.

The shortcut method above doesn't work for pivots, surface irrigation, or microirrigation. You can estimate net water application in inches per set for any irrigation system if you know the system's *flow rate, irrigated area* and *system efficiency.* The calculation is described in the following pages.

Finding Flow Rate
It's sometimes difficult to estimate flow rates for **surface irrigation systems,** but several methods are possible.

- To measure flow rates in a ditch or pipeline, you may be able to use one of the flow-measuring devices described later in this chapter.
- For furrow systems, portable furrow flow measuring devices are available.
- If you are using siphon tubes, you can look up the flow rate in a siphon tube head-discharge chart.
- You can catch the flow to a single furrow in a bucket of known capacity, and measure the time it takes to fill the bucket.
- If you know the total flow into a furrow system, you can divide this amount by the number of furrows to find the flow rate into each furrow.

To calculate flow rate for most **sprinkler systems,** you'll need to know the *average gpm per sprinkler.* For center pivots, flow varies along the length of lateral pipe, and you'll need to know the *gpm for the entire pivot.*

If your sprinkler system is relatively new and the nozzles have little wear, you can use the total design gpm of your system for a flow estimate. Be aware, however, that design numbers do not take into account increased flow (sometimes significant) due to nozzle wear and pressure variations. Divide the design gpm by the number of operating sprinklers on your sprinkler system to find the average gpm per sprinkler. For pivots, use the design gpm for the entire pivot.

A more accurate way to find the flow rate for your sprinkler system, especially if it's an older system, is to conduct a simple bucket test. (See the Conversions & Formulas section, p. 68.)

Finding Irrigated Area

For most surface irrigation systems, the irrigated area is simply the entire area of the field. For furrow systems, you can use the length and spacing of the furrows to estimate irrigated area. (See example below.)

For most sprinkler systems, find the area in square feet watered by one sprinkler, usually described as the distance in feet between sprinklers on the line multiplied by the distance in feet between mainline riser valves. Typical areas are 30 ft × 50 ft or 40 ft × 60 ft. See Figure 11 for an example. For pivots, use the entire swept area in acres and multiply by 43,560. (This converts acres to square feet.)

Calculating Net Water Application per Set

To calculate net water application in inches per set for any irrigation system, use the following general formula:

Net water application (inches) =

$$\frac{\text{set time (hours)} \times \text{flow rate (gpm)} \times 96.3 \times \text{system efficiency}}{\text{irrigated area (sq ft)}}$$

NOTE: 96.3 is a conversion factor.

Wheel line, hand line, end tow: Use the average flow rate (gpm) for one nozzle.

Example: 12-hour set, 8 gpm per sprinkler, 40 foot × 60 foot spacing, 65% system efficiency

$$\frac{12 \times 8 \times 96.3 \times 0.65}{40 \times 60} = 2.5 \text{ inches net water application per set}$$

Center pivot system: Use the total pivot flow.

Example: 50-hour rotation, 900 gpm, 130-acre field (= 5,662,800 ft²), 75% system efficiency

$$\frac{50 \times 900 \times 96.3 \times .75}{5,662,800} = 0.6 \text{ inches net water application per set}$$

NOTE: The wheel line example above uses the flow for one nozzle divided by the area covered by one nozzle. The pivot formula uses the flow for the entire pivot divided by the area covered by the entire pivot. The result is the same — inches per set.

Stationary big gun sprinkler: Use flow per sprinkler.

Example: 10-hour set, 78 gpm, 120 ft × 120 ft spacing, 50% system efficiency

$$\frac{10 \times 78 \times 96.3 \times 0.50}{120 \times 120} = 2.6 \text{ inches net water application per set}$$

Traveling big gun sprinkler: Use the following formula:

$$\text{Net water application} = \frac{\text{gpm} \times 1.6 \times \text{efficiency (\%)}}{S \times W}$$

where W = width between travel lanes in feet and S = travel speed in feet per minute (fpm).

Example: 300 feet between travel lanes, 0.4 fpm travel speed, 400 gpm, 60% system efficiency.

$$\frac{400 \times 1.6 \times 0.6}{0.4 \times 300} = 3.2 \text{ inches net water application}$$

Wild flood: Use total area flooded and total flow.

Example: Seven 24-hour days, 800 gpm flow, 40-acre field, 20% system efficiency

$$\frac{7 \times 24 \times 800 \times 96.3 \times 0.20}{40 \times 43,560} = 1.5 \text{ inches net water application}$$

Graded furrows: Use furrow length and spacing.

Example: 11-hour set, 10 gpm assumed flow per furrow, 660-foot-long × 3-foot-wide furrows, 50% system efficiency

$$\frac{11 \times 10 \times 96.3 \times 0.50}{3 \times 660} = 2.7 \text{ inches net water application}$$

Determining the Correct Set Time

Use the same formula to determine how long it takes to apply a desired amount of water by inserting the amount of water you *want to apply* for "net water application."

Set time hours =
$$\frac{\text{net water application (inches)} \times \text{irrigated area (sq ft)}}{\text{flow rate (gpm)} \times 96.3 \times \text{system efficiency}}$$

Example: Wheel line, 8 gpm per sprinkler, you want to apply 1.2 inches, 40 foot × 60 foot spacing, 65% system efficiency.

$$\frac{1.2 \times 40 \times 60}{8 \times 96.3 \times .65} = 5.8 \text{ hours. Round up to 6 hours.}$$

For surface irrigation systems, it may be easier to use the following formula:

Set time hours =
$$\frac{\text{gross water application (inches)} \times \text{area irrigated (acres)}}{\text{flow rate (cfs)}}$$

Surface Irrigation Example:

Graded borders, 1.2 cfs flow, 10 acre field, desired gross water application 1.5 inches.

Correct set time (hours) $= \dfrac{1.5 \times 10}{1.2} = 12.5 \text{ hours}$

Irrigating with Limited Water Supplies

When water supplies are short:

- *Don't over-irrigate.* Learn the AWC of your soils and the management allowable depletion (MAD), effective root depth, and critical growth stages of your crops.
- *Focus irrigation on critical growth stages.* Depending on the crop, you'll usually see one of two types of responses to drought stress:
  1. Seed crops, cereals, and oilseeds are most sensitive to drought stress during reproductive growth (flowering or seed formation), and relatively insensitive during vegetative growth. Make sure you irrigate enough at the onset of seed formation to carry the crop through seed fill.
  2. Perennial crops grown primarily for forage, and some root crops, are relatively insensitive to moderate drought stress for short periods throughout the growing season. They can recover from stress periods with little reduction in yield. Focus on irrigating during periods of maximum growth.
- *Irrigate early in the season.* Fill the root zone to field capacity before hot weather starts.
- *Leave room in the soil for precipitation.* Crop residue and cover crops help capture snow and rain, and reduce evaporation.
- *Aim for optimum rather than maximum yield,* i.e. the greatest yield with the least input.
- *Plant drought-tolerant crops,* or quick-maturing crops that require most of their water early in the season.
- *Reduce the amount of land you irrigate* or *reduce the amount of water you apply* over the whole irrigated area. As a rule of thumb, it's usually most economical to reduce acreage to the point where you can irrigate at about 80% of full irrigation.
- *Irrigate every other furrow,* switching furrows at each irrigation. You'll still get water to one side of each row, generally using far less water.

Measuring Flows

Flow measurement is essential for good management, making the most of limited water supplies, and maximizing profit, especially if you are purchasing water.

You can measure flowing water in an open channel or pipeline. You can also measure water at the point where sprinklers are applying it to the field, with a simple bucket test. (See Conversions and Formulas, p. 68.)

Measuring Open Channel Flow

Open channel methods generally rely on a structure such as a *weir, flume,* or *orifice* installed in the channel. These structures typically include one or more *staff gages* (also spelled *gauges*), installed either on the structure itself or in an adjacent still-ing well, to determine water depth. (A staff gage is simply a vertical staff — resembling an ordinary yardstick — marked with numbers that indicate water depth.) Using a table for the specific size and type of structure, you look up the measured depth and convert it to a flow rate. Higher cost but more ac-curate electronic measuring devices are now available that offer continuous flow measurement and recording.

Most open channel flow measuring devices only work under limited conditions. A structure suitable for a river or large canal will not be the best choice for a small ditch. Only a few of the most common methods for measuring flows are consid-ered here, for smaller canals, ditches, and farm turnouts. A comprehensive guide is the U.S. Bureau of Reclamation's *Water Measurement Manual,* available on the Internet at www.usbr.gov/pmts/hydraulics_lab/pubs/wmm/index.htm.

To ensure accuracy, the measuring site must meet a number of conditions:

• The ditch or canal must have a shallow grade with a relatively straight upstream segment and uniform cross-section, little turbulence, and quiet flow.

- Weirs require more slope than flumes or submerged orifices.
- The location must not cause sediment loading, debris buildup, or flooding of surrounding areas.

In selecting a water measurement structure, consider cost, accuracy, ease of measurement, construction and maintenance requirements, and state or local water laws and regulations.

Weirs are easy to construct, install, and use, but require enough ditch slope so that water can fall freely from the structure to the downstream water surface. In the case of *rectangular* and *trapezoidal* weirs, water flows through a sharp-edged rectangu-

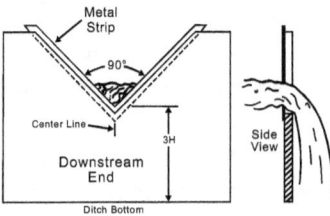

Figure 12. V-notch Weir

lar or trapezoidal notch. In the case of *v-notch* weirs, water flows through a sharp-edged (usually) 90 degree-angled notch. This weir is especially good at handling a wide range of flows.

FLOWS

Flumes are more complex structures than weirs, including a constricted throat section that requires careful construction and installation. Flumes are used where ditch and canal grades are relatively flat. They can still be relatively accurate even when submerged.

Parshall flumes, one of the most common types, require only about one-fourth of the ditch grade needed for weirs and can accommodate a wide range of flows. *Cutthroat flumes* are a "throatless" variation on the Parshall flume, resulting in simplified construction.

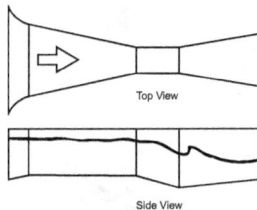

Figure 13. Parshall Flume

Ramp flumes (also known as *modified broad-crested weirs*) are accurate, cost less to build than most other devices, and are simpler to construct.

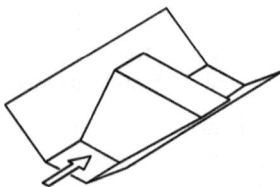

Figure 14. Ramp Flume

Submerged orifices are often used where ditch slope is insufficient for weirs. They generally cost less than weirs and can fit into limited spaces, but they are susceptible to trash build-up. Water flowing through an orifice is discharged below the downstream water surface. For this device to be accurate, it must be submerged. The *meter gate,* a type of submerged orifice, can be used for farm turnouts. The gate can be used to measure flow, closed to shut off flow, or positioned at various settings to reduce or increase flow.

Choosing, installing, and using weirs, flumes, and submerged orifices is not difficult. In order to get accurate results, though, you need to install these devices properly, maintain them regularly, use proper measuring techniques, and use the right calibration curves and tables. Your local NRCS, Extension, or conservation district office may be able to assist you.

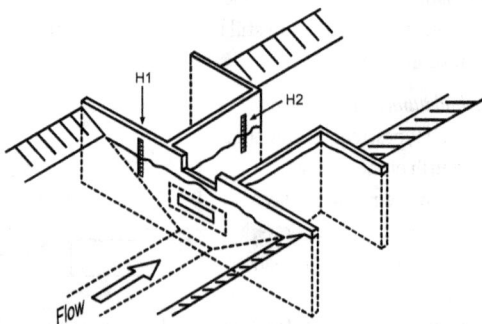

Figure 15. Submerged Orifice

Measuring Pipeline Flow

Flow in a pipeline can be measured very accurately if the correct measuring device is installed and used properly. These devices need periodic calibration and maintenance, and water must be relatively (in some cases, very) clean. Accurate measurement requires full pipe flow.

Pipeline flow is measured by either *intrusive* devices (located inside the pipe or inserted through the pipe wall) or *external* devices. Intrusive flow meters include *Venturi, nozzle,* and *orifice plate* meters which measure flow through a constriction within the pipe. All of these have no moving parts, require little maintenance in clean water, and are installed directly in the pipeline.

Propeller meters use a multi-blade propeller positioned inside the pipe. Propeller meters can pass some debris, but even moderate amounts of debris can foul the blades.

Pitot tubes are inserted into the side of a pipe. They require drilling a hole through the pipe (allowing the insertion of the tube), making them less convenient and common than propeller meters.

Non-intrusive (external) flow meters send ultrasonic or acoustic waves through a pipe and take very accurate measurements of Doppler shift or transit time to calculate flow rate. These devices are clamped onto the outside of the pipe wall and do not require inserting anything into the pipe, making them extremely quick and convenient to use. Several types of ultrasonic meters are currently on the market. They require some training for accurate measurement, and they are also costly: in the range of $1,500 to $10,000, although prices are dropping.

FLOWS

Know the Water Needs of Your Crops

This chapter explains

• how to track crop water use or evapotranspiration
• general irrigation guidelines and management allowable depletion values for some crops

Tracking Evapotranspiration (ET)

All irrigators should check their soil moisture and follow general recommendations like those in the crop data tables at the end of this chapter. **Most** irrigators will also find it worthwhile to track ET rates for their crops—the combined effect of evaporation from the soil surface and transpiration by plants. Soil moisture monitoring tells you how much water remains in the soil; tracking ET tells you how much water has been used up. ET is generally estimated from factors like temperature, wind speed, solar radiation, relative humidity, and crop type and stage.

It may seem odd to use ET estimates when you could directly measure moisture in the soil. Tracking ET has two advantages, though: It's often better than soil moisture monitoring for helping you *predict* when you'll need to irrigate. Second, tracking ET helps you decide *how much* water you need to apply.

Just as some irrigation managers rely entirely on soil moisture measurement, others simply track ET. The best approach, though, is three-pronged: monitoring soil moisture, following general watering recommendations for your crops, and tracking ET. Use soil moisture monitoring as a "reality check" to make sure that your ET calculations are on target.

The Checkbook Method

The allowable depletion balance is your safety cushion at any given time-the amount that can safely be depleted from the effective root zone without seriously affecting crop growth and yield. The usual method for tracking ET is known as the *checkbook* or *water balance* or *water budget* method. The idea is that you track water inputs and withdrawals from the soil, and plan your irrigation schedule, like balancing your checkbook or keeping a budget. The *beginning balance* is the amount of available water in the effective root zone at the start of the irrigation season or just after you've irrigated. The soil is considered *full* when it's at field capacity and *empty* when the allowable depletion balance reaches zero. Daily ET *withdraws* water from the effective root zone. Rainfall and irrigation *deposit* water into the root zone.

You can make the checkbook method as simple or complicated as you like, keeping track of inputs and outputs in a pocket notebook or on a computer spreadsheet. A detailed example is given below.

Publicly-Available ET Information

In many parts of the country, weather stations provide publicly-available daily crop water use reports, forecasts, and other general irrigation information. These weather stations use measurements of air temperature, relative humidity, wind speed, solar radiation, and sometimes other factors to calculate approximate ET.

Check the Internet, or your local paper or radio station for published "real time" ET information. If local information is available, find out if the weather station is close enough to provide reliable information for your location. You may find that the only information published is a "reference ET," commonly an ET value for alfalfa or grass. In this case, you'll need to use crop coefficient tables in order to convert these reference ET values to the ET rates for your crops. Your local NRCS or Extension office may be able to provide these tables. See the websites listed on pages v-viii for sources of this weather data.

Do-It-Yourself ET Information

If no publicly-available weather station data is available for your location, you might consider purchasing your own. Weather station prices generally start around $1,000 and go up to several thousand dollars. Software and a way to download information may cost extra. Weather stations have some disadvantages, including maintenance issues and lightning strikes that can destroy your investment in an instant.

Atmometers, also known as *evaporimeters* or *ET gauges*, estimate ET using a flat, porous ceramic disk that draws up water as evaporation dries the surface of the disk. Atmometers are generally cheaper than weather stations. Most provide reference ET values only, so you'll need crop coefficient tables to find an ET value that's correct for your crop.

Evaporation pans are open-top water containers, often standard metal washtubs. As water evaporates, the water level in the tub drops. Markings on the inside of the tub provide an estimate of available water remaining in the root zone. You can find guidelines and crop coefficient tables for evaporation pans on the internet, or your local NRCS or Extension office may be able to assist you in setting up and using one of these devices.

Using the Checkbook Method

To use the checkbook method, you find the management allowable depletion (MAD) for the crop at its current growth stage—the percentage of available water capacity (AWC) that can safely be depleted. You plan irrigations so they take place before this water is depleted, to avoid yield losses.

1. Determine Beginning Allowable Depletion Balance

Measure or estimate soil moisture levels when perennial crops begin to leaf out and at planting for annual crops. If soils are at field capacity, the allowable depletion balance equals AWC, and you can simply use a soil survey to estimate AWC in the depth of soil that you are managing. (See page 21, *Determining the Water-holding Capacity of Your Soils.*) The example that follows assumes that you are managing to the depth of the effective root zone.

Example:

Suppose spring barley at boot stage is on a field with Bozeman soils and the effective root depth is 2 to 3 feet. In the top 30 inches of soil depth, the *AWC* equals 5.32 inches at field capacity.

2. Find Management Allowable Depletion (MAD) for the Crop at its Current Growth Stage

The Crop Data Tables (pp. 51–57) show MAD values for some commonly irrigated crops. The effective root depth for many crops, especially annual or newly seeded perennial crops, will change significantly throughout the season.

Example:

For the barley example above, at the boot stage, MAD is 40 percent of AWC. So in the effective root zone—the top 30 inches of soil depth—MAD is 2.13 inches of water.

$$0.40 \times 5.32 = 2.13$$

3. Track ET and Precipitation

You'll need daily ET amounts (in inches) to subtract from the MAD. These ET values are entered into a table like the one on the following page.

In order to use precipitation effectively, you need to leave some room for it in the root zone. When it rains (or snows) add three quarters of that amount to the stored water in the soil. If less than 0.05 inches falls, ignore this amount. Remember that run-off and deep percolation are not useful moisture for the crop.

Example:

Suppose 0.4 inches of rain falls on June 24. Use 0.3 inches as the amount that enters the root zone.

4. Calculate Cumulative Water Use, and Recalculate Allowable Depletion Balance

Reduce soil water each day by the adjusted rainfall amount and the net irrigation amount. Increase soil water each day by the adjusted rainfall amount. Use the far right column to keep a running total: your safety cushion or *allowable depletion balance.*

There are many paper and pencil worksheets, computer spreadsheets, and online tools to help with checkbook irrigation scheduling. Some of these tools can be found by exploring the website links on pages vi-vii.

The example below starts when irrigation has raised the soil moisture to field capacity. At the beginning of this period, 2.13 inches of water are available to be safely depleted from the effective root zone. Six days of adjusted ET are subtracted and one day of rainfall is added

	ET	Rainfall	Net Irrigation	Allowable Depletion Balance
Date	−	+	+	2.13
21-Jun	0.25			1.88
22-Jun	0.12			1.76
23-Jun	0.25			1.51
24-Jun	0.25	0.3		1.56
25-Jun	0.3			1.26
26-Jun	0.3			0.96

On June 26 the allowable depletion balance is 0.96 inches in the effective root zone, meaning that 0.96 inches is available to be safely depleted.

5. Decide When and How Much to Irrigate

Using the checkbook method, you can plan to irrigate before your allowable depletion balance reaches zero. To determine the number of days until irrigation is needed, divide your current allowable depletion balance by the estimated daily ET. In the example above, suppose ET will continue at 0.3 inches per day. In this case, the 0.96 inches in the effective root zone on June 26 will be almost completely depleted in three days, or on June 29.

Continuing the example above, suppose you apply a net irrigation of 2.04 inches on June 30. Filling in ET values for June 27-30, the balance sheet would look like this:

Date	ET	Rainfall	Net Irrigation	Allowable Depletion Balance
	−	+	+	2.13
21-Jun	0.25			1.88
22-Jun	0.12			1.76
23-Jun	0.25			1.51
24-Jun	0.25	0.3		1.56
25-Jun	0.3			1.26
26-Jun	0.3			0.96
27-Jun	0.35			0.61
28-Jun	0.27			0.34
29-Jun	0.25			0.09
30-Jun	0.36		2.04	1.77

❗Caution: When you irrigate, bring the soil moisture no higher than field capacity. Amounts over field capacity are not available to the crop because this water is quickly lost through deep percolation or runoff.

In the example above, suppose that no rain is expected for the next week and that you have decided to bring the soil moisture to field capacity. Use one of the following two formulas to determine the correct set time to fill the effective root zone with the appropriate amount of water. The first formula is convenient for many sprinkler systems; the second formula is handy for many surface irrigation systems.

Correct set time (hours) =
$$\frac{\text{net water application (inches)} \times \text{irrigated area (sq ft)}}{\text{flow rate (gpm)} \times 96.3 \times \text{system efficiency (\%)}}$$

Correct set time (hours) =
$$\frac{\text{gross water application (inches)} \times \text{area irrigated (acres)}}{\text{flow rate (cfs)}}$$

In the first formula above, *system efficiency* is the percentage of water applied that actually becomes available to the plant roots. (See page 27–28)

Gross water applied × system efficiency = net water applied

Sprinkler example (first formula):
Wheel line, 8 gpm nozzles, 40 ft by 60 ft spacing, 65% efficiency. Following the example above, suppose the allowable depletion balance has reached 0.09 inches and you need a net water application of 2.04 inches to reach field capacity.

$$\frac{2.04 \times 40 \times 60}{8 \times 96.3 \times .65} = 9.78 \text{ (round up to 10-hour sets)}$$

Surface example (second formula):
Graded borders, 1.2 cfs flow, 10 acre field, desired gross water application 1.5 inches.

$$\text{Correct set time (hours)} = \frac{1.5 \times 10}{1.2} = 12.5 \text{ hours}$$

After calculating the set time, check to make sure that the application rate does not exceed the soil intake rate. For example, suppose that irrigation is taking place on a silt loam soil, at an application rate of about 0.32 inches per hour. Table 2 on page 13 shows that the intake rate for sprinklers on medium texture soils (including silt loams) is 0.5 to 0.7 inches. Runoff should be minimal.

A Note on Overwatering

If you are living by the wasteful rule "When in doubt, irrigate," consider that over-irrigating can:

- drown crop root systems, depleting air and encouraging disease
- leach nutrients, especially nitrogen, below the root zone
- send nutrients into the groundwater
- reduce root growth by cooling the soil
- cause waterlogging and salt build-up in the root zone
- reduce crop quality and yield
- waste energy and money

Crop Data Tables

All irrigators should know general irrigation guidelines for the crops they are growing. Different crops can tolerate different soil moisture depletion levels, and most crops are especially sensitive to insufficient water during a certain growth stage. Moisture stress during this critical stage can cause an irreversible loss of yield or quality.

Management allowable depletion (MAD) is defined as the percentage of available water (AWC) that can safely be depleted without seriously affecting plant growth and development. The Crop Data Tables (starting on page 51) show MAD values for a number of common crops and provide some other general irrigation guidelines for these crops. For more detailed information on irrigation management of these and other crops, contact your local NRCS or Cooperative Extension Service office.

As a general rule of thumb, recommended MAD values are typically 25 to 40 percent for high-value, shallow-rooted crops;

50 percent for deep-rooted crops; and 60 to 65 percent for low-value deep-rooted crops. For deep-rooted crops, recommended MAD values are typically about 40 percent for fine-textured (clayey) soils, 50 percent for medium-textured (loamy) soils, and 60 percent for coarse-textured (sandy) soils.

! **Caution: The following tables give only general recommendations and average values. The guidelines may need to be adjusted for your own situation, including your local climate and soil texture. Effective root depth is generally about one half of unrestricted potential rooting depth. (See page 24 on finding your actual effective root zone.) If your actual rooting depth is restricted, reduce the effective root depth in the tables accordingly. Always proceed cautiously, watch carefully how your crops are responding, and make adjustments as needed.**

Table 8. Crop Data

Crop	Effective Root Depth (ft)	MAD[1] (% of AWC)	Critical Growth Stage	General Guides
Alfalfa				
Established stands	4.0	50%	Early spring and immediately after cuttings	Adequate water is needed between cuttings. Avoid over-irritation. Irrigation to effective root depth should be done in spring and fall where precipitation is not adequate.
1st cut – 2nd cut				
2nd cut – 3rd cut				
New seedings				
Emergence to 1st cut	0.5-1.5	50-65%	Seedling	
Alfalfa-Grass				
Established stands	2.0-4.0	50%	Early spring and immediately after cuttings	Same as alfalfa.
1st cut – 2nd cut				
2nd cut – 3rd cut				
New seedings				
Seedling to 1st cut	0.5-1.0		Seedling	

[1]The percent of available water capacity that can be depleted by the crop without causing yield or quality loss due to moisture stress.

CROPS / ET

51

Crop	Effective Root Depth (ft)	MAD[1] (% of AWC)	Critical Growth Stage	General Guides
Beans, Dry				
4-leaf	0.8-1.0	40%	Early bloom, pod formation	Very sensitive to over-irrigation. Yield reduced if water is short at bloom and pod set. Last irrigation when earliest pods start maturing.
First flower	1.5			
First pod set	2.0-2.5			
Corn, Grain				
Emergence to tasseling	0.5-2.0	50-60%	Tasseling, silking, until grain becomes firm	Sensitive to over-irrigation. Needs adequate moisture from germination to dent stage. Restricted moisture shortly after emergence encourages tillering. Moisture shortage after hard dough stage does not affect yield.
12-leaf to silking	2.0-3.0*	50%		
Blister kernel to dough	3.0-3.5*	50-60%		

*Corn effective root depth will be shallower in humid climates.

52

Grapes

Established vines			
Shoot growth	3.0-4.0	40%	During rapid shoot growth & cell division in berries, summer cell expansion in berries	Start season with soil profile full at effective root depth. Avoid over-irrigating.
Flowering			
Ripening		50%	

Grass For Pasture/Hay

Established stands	1.5-3.5	50-60%	First 3 months of establishment	During establishment 50% of MAD must be maintained to the effective root depth. Use light, frequent irrigations.
New seedings				
Vegetative	0.0-0.5	40%		
Reproductive: flowering	0.5-1.5	50-60%		
Maturity	1.5-3.0			

53

Crop	Effective Root Depth (ft)	MAD[1] (% of AWC)	Critical Growth Stage	General Guides
Onions, Dry				
Establishment	1.0	40%	Transplanting, bulb enlargement	Apply frequent, light irrigations to keep soil moist. Cease irrigating once bulbs are full size and tops begin falling.
Bulb formation		30%		
Bulb growth				
Orchard, Fruits				
Tree size 3´ x 10´	2.0	50% at 2-ft level. 1st irrigation should fill root zone	Flowering to 4 weeks after bloom, fruit set, last 2-4 weeks before harvest	Some fruits are sensitive to stress during the last two weeks to harvest. Reduce orchard water use by controlling weeds and suppressing cover crop growth.
Tree size 6´ x 13´	3.0-3.5			
Tree size 12´ x 18´	4-5			

Potatoes

	Effective Root Depth	MAD	Critical Growth Stage	General Guides
Vegetative	0.5-1.0		Flowering, tuber formation and growth	Sensitive to over-irrigation. Water should not stand around tubers. Light, frequent irrigation best. Reduced tuber quality if plants go into serious moisture stress. Last irrigation 3-4 weeks before harvest.
Reproductive: tuber initiation and growth	1.0-2.0	35%		
Maturation	1.5-2.0	50%		

Crop	Effective Root Depth (ft)	MAD[1] (% of AWC)	Critical Growth Stage	General Guides
Small Grains				
Vegetative	0.5-2.0	60%	Boot, bloom, and early heading	Restrict moisture early in year to encourage stooling prior to boot stage. Irrigate to field capacity. Last irrigation at mild to dough stage. Irrigating after late dough may decrease yield.
Boot through flowering	2.0-3.0	40%		
Milk to soft dough	3.0-3.5	60%		

CROPS / ET

55

Crop	Effective Root Depth (ft)	MAD[1] (% of AWC)	Critical Growth Stage	General Guides
Soybeans				
Vegetative	0.8-1.0	60-65%	Early bloom, pod formation	Yield reduced if water is short at bloom and pod set. Last irrigation when earliest pods start maturing.
First flower to first pod	1.5	50-60%		
First pod to maturity	2.0	50-65%		
Sugar Beets				
Vegetative: first 5 weeks after emergence	0.0-1.0	50%	From seedling to root enlargement (post thinning)	Irrigate frequently and lightly during early season to ensure germination and seedling growth. Later in season avoid irrigating when crop simply shows signs of mid-afternoon wilt. Excessive irrigation lowers sugar content.
Vegetative: mid-May to mid-September	1.5-2.0			
Maturation: mid-August to harvest	2.0-3.0			

Table 9. Recommended Management Allowable Depletion (MAD or % of AWC) for Some Additional Crops Assumed to be Growing in Loamy Soils

Crop	Crop growth stage			
	Establishment	Vegetative	Flowering yield formation	Ripening maturity
Alfalfa seed	50	60	50	80
Beans, green	40	40	40	40
Citrus	50	50	50	50
Corn, seed	50	50	50	50
Corn, sweet	50	40	40	40
Cranberries	40	50	40	40
Garlic	30	30	30	30
Grass seed	50	50	50	50
Lettuce	40	50	40	20
Milo	50	50	50	50
Mint	40	40	40	50
Nursery stock	50	50	50	50
Peas	50	50	50	50
Peanuts	40	50	50	50
Safflower	50	50	50	50
Spinach	25	25	25	25
Sunflower	50	50	50	50
Tobacco	40	40	40	50
Vegetables				
1 to 2 ft root depth	35	30	30	35
3 to 4 ft root depth	35	40	40	40

Adapted from *NRCS Irrigation Guide,* USDA Natural Resources Conservation Service, 1997.

❗Caution: Fine textured soils can reduce MAD values given in this table. Use the MAD values for your specific soils if your NRCS or Extension office can provide them.

Efficient Surface Irrigation

This chapter explains

• several surface irrigation methods
• some ways to improve surface irrigation efficiency
• some erosion control techniques for surface irrigation

In general, surface irrigation stores large volumes of water in the soil and uses water less efficiently than sprinklers or microirrigation. While some surface irrigation systems achieve high efficiencies, most of these systems allow only limited control. Light, shallow watering is often impossible. Distribution uniformity can be poor, with some parts of the field being over-watered and other parts being underwatered. Erosion is often a concern, especially when water is flowing over sloping terrain.

Management for surface irrigation systems is generally based on some combination of the three basic approaches described in the preceding chapters: monitoring soil moisture, follow-ing general crop-specific guidelines, and using a version of the checkbook method to track ET. Because of the limited control inherent in many surface irrigation systems, soil moisture monitoring is especially important, as a "reality check" for what's happening beneath the soil's surface. Inefficiency, although com-mon, is not inevitable. With skill and attention, most surface irrigation systems can be managed quite efficiently.

Surface Irrigation Methods

Level Basins, Borders

Level basin systems allow water to flow over a nearly-level field and into a basin surrounded by dikes or levees. These systems distribute water uniformly and keep surface runoff to a mini-mum. High-velocity flows are normally recommended for efficient management, flooding the basin to the desired depth as quickly as possible. Level basins are somewhat susceptible to overwatering, especially when they are managed (mistakenly) like graded border strips.

Level Furrow

Level furrows have blocked ends, causing water to be contained and ponded within the furrows. These systems are easy to manage, can achieve very high efficiency, distribute water very uniformly, allow precise control over irrigation amounts, and reduce or eliminate runoff. On the other hand, level furrow irrigation is quite labor-intensive and is not well-suited to soils with high intake rate and low water-holding capacity.

Graded Borders

Parallel dikes or ridges divide a field into uniform-width, slightly-sloping *border strips*. Water flows into these strips one at a time. Efficient irrigation requires a properly-sized stream, one that irrigates the entire strip without causing heavy runoff at the lower end. Graded borders allow the use of water that is high in suspended sediments. On the other hand, this method requires skill and attention to avoid overwatering.

Graded Furrow

Water flows through slightly-sloping furrows. Graded furrow systems can use water that is high in suspended sediments, and properly-managed systems achieve high application uniformity. On the other hand, erosion is a common concern, tailwater usually results, management requirements can be high, and the upper end of the field must sometimes be overwatered in order to deliver enough water to the lower end. High-velocity flows tend to improve uniformity. Soil intake rate, furrow spacing, and field length are all critical variables.

Contour Ditch

In this method, irrigation ditches run along the contour. Water overflows the banks of the ditch and moves down the slope as a uniform (at least in theory) sheet, until it is collected in the next ditch. Contour ditch systems are inexpensive to establish but application uniformity is often problematic. These systems also pose erosion risks.

Wild Flood

Water is allowed to flow over the land without the use of furrows, borders or other structures. Wild flooding is generally the least water-efficient surface irrigation method.

Improving the Efficiency of Surface Irrigation Systems

Below are some techniques for improving the efficiency of surface irrigation systems. Some of these recommendations are specific to graded furrow systems.

Decrease Set Time or Irrigation Frequency

Use the techniques on pages 28–34 to make sure you know your approximate net water application per set. Monitor soil moisture, follow general crop-specific irrigation guidelines, and use some version of the checkbook method to track ET. You may find that you can reduce your set time or wait longer between irrigations.

Carefully time your sets and watch the water closely during irrigation. Experiment with different stream sizes and set times to achieve uniform infiltration and minimum runoff.

About 24 hours after irrigation, probe various parts of the field to check for soil moisture, infiltration uniformity, and deep percolation.

Land Leveling

Precision surface grading and land-leveling can greatly improve the uniformity and efficiency of most surface irrigation systems.

Gated Pipe

Gated pipe is plastic or aluminum pipe with many small adjustable gates, generally spaced 18 to 24 inches apart. Once the pipe is filled with water, the gates are opened one at a time, applying water in the desired pattern. Gated pipe eliminates leakage, percolation losses, and evaporation associated with ditches, and greatly increases control over the whole irrigation process.

Figure 16. Gated Pipe

Surge Irrigation

Surge irrigation is one of the best ways to improve the efficiency of surface irrigation while reducing labor requirements and increasing control over the irrigation process. Water is applied intermittently to furrows or border strips, alternating between two parts of the field and creating alternating wetting and "resting" times during each surge.

Normally, a battery powered, timer-controlled valve controls the direction of the irrigation flow, automating the process. The first surge lightly wets soils in one part of the field. Then the valve diverts water to the other side of the field. Each subsequent surge causes deeper infiltration as water advances farther down the field, until the water has advanced all the way to the end of the field.

Surge irrigation generally waters a field in the same number of hours as conventional approaches, but using far less water. By gradually wetting soils, surge irrigation conserves water and energy, improves infiltration uniformity, decreases deep percolation and runoff, and reduces erosion.

Poly Pipe

Poly pipe is flexible tubing, ranging from 6 to 15 mils thick and 8 to 22 inches in diameter. It comes in 300–1300 foot rolls, is flat when purchased, and inflates as it is filled with water. Poly pipe behaves similarly to gated pipe, but is flexible instead of being rigid. You can cut holes or install gates at any interval you desire—delivering water to furrows without the need for siphon tubes. Among its many advantages, poly pipe can follow the edges of irregularly-shaped fields and can make 90-degree turns. It cannot move water uphill, however. The tubing is gradually damaged by the sun's ultraviolet rays and must be replaced periodically. With careful use, though, it can last several seasons.

Cutback of Inflow

When the water has nearly reached the end of the furrow, the inflow rate is reduced, increasing uniformity of infiltration along the furrow length and reducing runoff.

Cablegation

This method basically automates the process of cutback irrigation. A plug inserted in a gated pipe is pushed slowly through the pipe by water pressure. The plug is restrained by a small cable or rope attached to a braking device. The speed of the cable controls the time of set and depth of application. As the plug moves past each gate, water gushes out. Flow gradually reduces as the plug moves farther down the pipe and the water level inside the pipe gradually drops below the level of the gate opening.

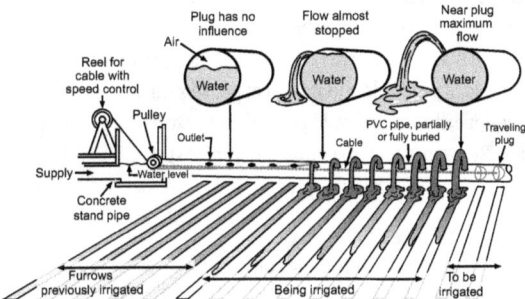

Figure 17. Cablegation Arrangement (Adapted from *NRCS Irrigation Guide*, USDA Natural Resources Conservation Service, 1997).

Furrow Diking

Small earthen dams are created across the furrows, every few feet along the length of the furrow. Water is ponded between the dikes, improving infiltration and reducing runoff. On the other hand, furrow diking increases labor and cost.

Modified Slope

In one method, furrow slope is gradually reduced throughout the entire length of the field. In another method, furrows are graded in the upper part of the field and level in the lower part. Either way, the result is improved uniformity of infiltration along the length of the furrow and reduced erosion.

Tailwater Reuse (Pumpback)

A tailwater reuse (pumpback) facility ordinarily includes tailwater collection ditches, a pumping plant with sump, pipelines, and a holding pond. Most of the runoff or tailwater is returned to the head of the same field or to another field for reuse. This method reduces runoff and conserves water, but runoff may contain high levels of nutrients and pesticides.

Maximum Allowable Stream Size for Furrow Irrigation

Furrow erosion is a major problem on highly erodible soils with slopes as flat as one percent or even less. Soils may erode if the furrow velocity exceeds about 0.5 feet per second. Regardless of furrow slope, flow rate should generally not exceed 50 gallons per minute. Recommended maximum allowable stream sizes are:

$Q = 15 \div S$ erosion resistant soils

$Q = 12.5 \div S$ average soils

$Q = 10 \div S$ moderately erodible soils

$Q = 5 \div S$ highly erodible soils (This value can range from 3 to 9, depending on erodibility of soils.)

where:

Q = gpm per furrow

S = slope in percent

Example: Moderately erodible soils, 2 percent slope. Stream size should not exceed 10 ÷ 2 = 5 gpm per furrow.

Other Erosion Control Techniques

Change furrow length or grade

Shorten the length of the run or reduce irrigation grades to allow reduced furrow inflow rate.

Change crops

Use higher residue-producing crops or ones that provide permanent cover.

Change tillage practices

Use reduced tillage or no-till practices to maintain higher rates of residue on the soil surface.

Improve surface residue

Place straw in the furrows by hand or equipment.

Install vegetative filter strips

A temporary or permanent vegetative filter strip at the head or lower end of the field helps filter out sediments as well as chemicals (fertilizers and pesticides).

Redistribute collected sediment

Annually haul and re-spread collected eroded soil.

Use polyacrylamide (PAM)

When added to furrow inflow water, PAM reduces erosion by stabilizing soil in the bottom and sides of the furrow and by causing suspended sediments to aggregate. Use only PAMs that are:

- officially labeled for erosion control by your state.

- designated as "water soluble," "linear," or "non-crosslinked."

- not too old. Most forms have a shelf life of only about one year.

- anionic (negatively charged). Cationic (positively charged) PAMs can harm the environment.

- moderate to high in molecular weight (typically 12 to 15 Mg/mole).

- less than 0.05 percent free acrylamide monomer (AMD) by weight.

Efficient Sprinkler Irrigation

This chapter explains

• several sprinkler irrigation methods
• several ways to improve sprinkler system efficiency
• some ways to control runoff

Compared to surface irrigation, sprinkler irrigation generally uses water more efficiently and allows a greater degree of control. On the other hand, distribution uniformity can be a problem, especially in windy areas.

Some sprinkler systems, such as wheel lines and hand lines, apply water in one location for a period of time. In some ways, these *periodic move* systems resemble surface irrigation methods. They store fairly large volumes of water in the soil during each set, and each part of the field is watered infrequently—generally every several days. Because so much water is stored in the soil, periodic move sprinkler systems have a built-in margin for error. On the other hand, overwatering is an ever-present danger.

Other sprinkler systems, such as linear move systems and center pivots, move more or less continuously. These *continuous move* systems store low volumes of water in the soil during each set. Each part of the field is watered briefly and frequently—perhaps every two or three days. The irrigator has a high degree of control over the way water is applied. On the other hand, because water applications are light, the margin for error is smaller than with a periodic move system. Soil moisture must be managed carefully throughout the season in order to avoid soil moisture shortages.

Sprinkler irrigators generally have more flexibility and management options than surface irrigators. In many cases it is possible to calculate and regulate quite accurately the volumes of water being applied. Management is generally based on some combination of the three basic approaches described in the preceding chapters: monitoring soil moisture, following general crop-specific irrigation guidelines, and using a version of the checkbook method to track ET.

Sprinkler Irrigation Methods

Hand Move Laterals (Also known as *hand line* or *hand move* systems)
These systems consist of portable aluminum or plastic pipelines, usually 20 to 40 feet long, with risers and sprinkler heads. These lateral pipelines are connected manually to a mainline pipe, by quick couplers.

Side Roll Laterals (Also known as *wheel line* systems)
These systems are similar to hand move laterals except that large wheels are mounted on the lateral pipe, which functions as an axle. The wheels move the lateral by rolling and are usually powered by a small gasoline engine.

Hose-Fed Laterals (Also known as *pull* laterals)
A few sprinkler heads (usually less than six) are mounted on lightweight flexible plastic or rubber hose. The hose is pulled by hand to the desired location. In one new system that is well-suited to pastures, low-volume sprinkler heads are mounted inside durable "pods" at 50-foot intervals along up to 660 feet of flexible polyethylene hose. The pods are towed into place using a 4-wheeled all-terrain vehicle.

Stationary Gun (Also known as *gun, big gun*)
A large, rotating, single-impact-type sprinkler head discharges large volumes of water in a circular pattern. The sprinkler is moved either by hand or with a tractor. Application uniformity is fair to poor, especially in windy areas and along the sides and ends of fields. Because of the large droplet size, compaction and surface sealing are concerns on low-intake soils.

Traveling Gun (Also known as *traveler, gun, big gun*)
These gun-type sprinkler systems are connected to the water
supply by a flexible hose and are self-moving, pulled or reeled
along a straight line by a water piston, water turbine-powered
winch, or small gasoline engine.

Boom Sprinklers

A boom containing several impact sprinklers or spray heads
rotates around a central swivel joint. The boom remains at one
location until adequate water is applied, then is towed to a new
location with a tractor. Boom systems are inexpensive but have
poor uniformity of application in windy areas.

Traveling Boom

These self-moving systems resemble traveling guns but use a
(rotating or fixed) boom containing several nozzles. Traveling
booms are inexpensive and apply water more uniformly than
traveling guns, but have generally high maintenance requirements.

Fixed Solid Set

Lateral pipes are installed in a pattern allowing the entire field to
be watered without moving the pipes. Ordinarily, a control valve
activates one group of sprinklers at a time, until the entire field
is irrigated. Solid set systems eliminate the labor associated with
moving pipe, and they are easily automated.

Center Pivot

A lateral supported by wheeled towers rotates continuously
(or by frequent starts and stops) around a fixed pivot point at
the center of the field. Application uniformity is usually high,
labor requirements are low, and pressure requirements are often
low too, allowing the use of smaller pumps and motors. On
the other hand, because water applications are light, pivots are
sometimes incapable of "catching up" if an irrigator falls behind

and soils become too dry. New center pivot users commonly overestimate application rates and underwater their crops.

Linear Move (Also known as *lateral* move)
Linear move systems, like pivots, are self-moving, with the lateral pipe supported by wheeled towers, trusses, and cables. Linear systems move in a straight line, and irrigate a rectangular field. Like pivots, linear move systems can be equipped with drop tubes and various spray heads to reduce wind drift and evaporative losses.

Low energy precision application (LEPA) & Low Pressure In Canopy (LPIC) systems

LEPA systems are generally center pivot or linear move systems that apply water at low pressure via drop tubes, directly onto the ground surface below the crop canopy. This method uses water extremely efficiently, reducing wind drift and evaporation losses to near zero. Because application rates can be quite high (up to 30 inches per hour), erosion is a concern on sloping fields (above one percent) or those with low intake rates. LPIC systems are similar to LEPA systems, but apply water a little higher above the ground, within the crop canopy. While slightly less water-efficient than LEPA systems, LPIC systems also cause less erosion.

Improving the Efficiency of Sprinkler Systems

Maintain Your Equipment

Poorly maintained systems often waste water, with *worn nozzles* and *leaks* topping the list of problems. Both problems increase application rates and cause uniformity problems that may force irrigators to resort to longer set times, thus decreasing irrigation efficiency.

Change Sprinkler Heads or Nozzles

Periodic move systems on hilly terrain often benefit from *flow-control* nozzles. These nozzles deliver a constant volume of water under varying pressures, improving application uniformity and sometimes allowing reduced set time.

Among the dozens of new sprinkler options for pivot and linear move systems are *spinners* or *wobblers* that produce larger droplets and reduce wind drift. *Dual spray heads* allow for different spray options for different crop stages and rooting depths. *Spray plates* can be replaced to allow for different spray patterns.

Use an Irrigation Timer

An irrigation timer ($50–$300) can save labor, energy, and water by shutting off your sprinkler system after the correct amount of water has been applied.

Decrease Set Time or Irrigation Frequency

Monitor soil moisture, follow general crop-specific irrigation guidelines, and use some version of the checkbook method to track ET. Calculate your system's net water application per set. You may find that you can reduce your set time or wait longer between irrigations.

Follow Your Design Specifications

Make sure you are running your irrigation system at the pressure and flow rate for which it was designed. When pressure is lower or higher than the system was designed to handle, distribution uniformity will be compromised. Dry spots and too-wet spots in the field can decrease crop yield, uniformity, and quality, and also increase the probability of leaching fertilizers. The grower tends to over-apply water everywhere to make up the difference in the dry spots.

SPRINKLER

71

Controlling Runoff

If a sprinkler system's application rate is greater than the soil intake rate, the result is runoff. In the worst case, excess water collects on the surface, then moves down slope and off the field. Even if runoff remains on the field, application is no longer uniform. Runoff wastes water, energy, topsoil, fertilizer, and may carry sediment and chemicals into nearby surface waters.

If your sprinkler system is worn or incorrectly designed for your soils, it may be contributing to runoff. Worn or oversized sprinkler nozzles put on more water at lower pressures than new nozzles correctly sized for your soils. Low-pressure pivot and linear move systems can cause runoff if not designed correctly or if used on soils with low intake rates.

Below are some suggestions for avoiding runoff:

• Avoid irrigating on bare soil. If it's necessary, reduce set times to a minimum.
• Leave the soil surface rough to create many small surface storage areas. This gives water time to infiltrate.
• Leave crop residue on the soil surface to slow water movement.
• For rolling cropland, strips of permanent grass cover between fields will catch water and sediment.

A Tip for Hand Move and Wheel Line Systems

Consider moving every other riser (or set location) as you go across the field in one direction, then hitting the missed locations as you come back in the other direction. This will:

• decrease the probability of surface runoff;
• decrease potential losses of water to deep percolation;
• get water to most of the field more often, decreasing the potential for crop stress; and
• help with the logistics of trying to move the system all the way back across the field empty to start over again.

Efficient Microirrigation

This chapter explains

• several microirrigation methods
• advantages and disadvantages of microirrigation systems
• some ways to improve microirrigation system efficiency
• how to estimate required hours of operation

Microirrigation systems deliver water through low-volume, low-pressure devices such as drip emitters, micro spray and sprinkler heads, and bubblers. These systems generally apply water at very low rates and apply it frequently (often daily). Microirrigation is commonly used to irrigate windbreaks, vegetables, berries, grapes, fruit, citrus and nut orchards, nursery stock, and landscape and ornamental plantings.

Microirrigation systems may either be *above-ground* or *buried*. Some above-ground systems are disposable, used for only one or two seasons, while others are re-used for many seasons. Likewise, buried drip systems may either be *one-crop* or *permanent*.

Microirrigation systems give the irrigator a high degree of control over the way water is applied, and typically cause little or no erosion. On the other hand, these systems must be designed, installed, and maintained carefully. Many systems are prone to clogging and require very clean water. Because water applications are so light, little water is stored in the soil, shrinking the irrigator's margin for error.

Microirrigation Methods

Drip Emitters

Drip emitters (also known as *point source* emitters) drip or trickle water from a single point or opening. *Orifice emitters* discharge water through a narrow passageway. *Turbulent flow emitters* direct water through a wider and "tortuous" (crooked or zigzagging) path that creates turbulence to reduce pressure with less clogging. Some emitters are pressure-compensating, discharging at a nearly constant rate over a range of pressures. Most drip emitters are designed to be used above-ground.

Line-Source Emitter Systems

(Also known as *drip tape, drip tubing,* and similar names)
Line-source emitters are basically flexible tubing with uni-formly-spaced emitter points. Some drip tape emits water through small laser-drilled holes. Other drip tape designs (*turbulent flow* tape) include equally-spaced tortuous path emitter devices within the tubing. Some drip tape is designed for above-ground use, while other types may be buried.

Basin Bubblers

More commonly seen in urban and residential settings than in agriculture, basin bubblers apply water in a small fountain, and a small basin or depression in the surrounding soil holds the water to allow infiltration.

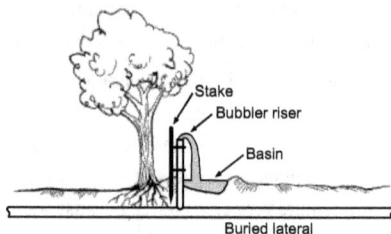

Figure 18. Basin Bubbler

Spray or Mini-Sprinklers

(Also known as *microspray* or *microsprinkler systems*)
Mini-sprinkler systems emit droplets from small, low-pressure heads. Some have spinners, while others contain no moving parts. Compared to drip emitters, they wet a wider area and are less prone to clogging, since water moves through them at a high velocity. High-discharge microsprinklers have larger diameter passageways and are especially resistant to clogging.

Advantages & Disadvantages

Microirrigation systems have many advantages:

- Frequent irrigation makes possible a high degree of control over the timing and amount of water applied.
- Well designed, installed, and maintained systems are highly efficient in their use of water, retaining as much as 85 to 95 percent of applied water in the root zone of plants.
- Precise water delivery to the immediate vicinity of plant roots reduces the risks of erosion, surface runoff, deep percolation, and leaching nutrients or pesticides to groundwater.
- Distribution can be highly uniform, reducing the need to over-water some parts of the field to avoid underwatering other parts.
- Yield and quality improvements have been shown for many crops.
- Fertilizer can be injected in precise amounts, directly to the root zone, and at the right times for optimal growth.
- Smaller pumping plants are often required, using up to 50 percent less energy than conventional sprinkler systems.
- Fewer tractor trips across the field are needed, since chemicals can be injected through the irrigation system.
- The surface stays drier, reducing weed growth and muddy conditions that complicate using vehicles in the field.
- Drip systems apply almost no water onto leaves, stems, or fruit—an advantage in avoiding certain plant diseases.
- Microirrigation systems are easily automated, starting and stopping at pre-set intervals or responding directly to soil moisture measuring devices.
- Microirrigation works well on irregularly shaped fields, steep slopes, and soils with low infiltration rates or low water-holding capacity.
- Salinity problems are reduced, for three reasons: (1) More continuously wet soil keeps salts diluted. (2) Salts move to the outer edges of the wetted soil area, away from plant roots. (3) Salts have little or no chance of being absorbed through the leaves.

Some disadvantages of microirrigation systems are:

• Microirrigation systems require more intensive and technical management than conventional surface or sprinkler systems, and also require new management skills and attitudes.

• Microirrigation systems are among the most expensive to purchase and install, costing $900 to $1300 per acre, or more.

• High quality irrigation water is required to prevent clogging, since water is delivered through small openings. Filtration and regular flushing are required, and chemical injection is usually needed to control biological and chemical sources of clogging.

• Animals, machinery, and foot traffic can cause leaks in above-ground tubing. Rodents, insects, and root intrusion can cause leaks and other damage to buried systems.

• Plants often have restricted roots, reducing their ability to withstand dry period without water.

• The irrigator's margin for error is reduced in hot dry conditions, since precise amounts of water are applied and stored in the soil. The water supply must be dependable. Regular inspections and troubleshooting are a must, and equipment problems must be repaired promptly.

• Although some salinity problems are reduced, salt accumulation can still be a problem since water applications are often insufficient to flush salts below the root zone. In severe cases, a sprinkler or surface irrigation system may need to be used to leach salts below the root zone.

Improving the Efficiency of Microirrigation Systems

Properly designed, installed, and maintained microirrigation systems are, in general, highly efficient in their use of water and energy.

• Check frequently for leaks. These are usually easy to spot in surface drip and microsprinkler systems, but harder to detect in subsurface systems. Watch your flowmeters: leaks cause increased flow and decreased pressure.

- Find and address causes of clogging. If you just install new emitters as a quick fix, clogging problems inevitably recur. Watch your flowmeters: clogging causes decreased flow downstream from clogs and increased pressure upstream.

- Check for plugged filter screens. Backflush as needed, and undo and clean any screens that are plugged.

- Flush lateral lines regularly—about every two weeks is a common interval.

- Inject chlorine or acid as needed, to control mineral precipitation and biological contamination. See the *Equipment Maintenance* half of this book for specific recommendations.

- Avoid excessive backflushing that wastes water and energy and creates water disposal problems.

Hours of Operation

Microirrigation systems are managed quite differently from other irrigation systems. Irrigation is frequent, maintaining a nearly constant, high level of soil moisture. Microirrigation often focuses water in the root zone of individual plants, instead of applying a uniform layer of water across an entire field. Typically, flowmeters measure the volume of water flowing through the system, and soil moisture monitoring is used to confirm the adequacy of moisture levels.

Despite these differences, management is generally based on some combination of the three basic approaches described in the preceding chapters: monitoring soil moisture, following general crop-specific irrigation guidelines, and using a version of the checkbook method to track ET.

Because irrigations are so frequent, the checkbook-style calculations do not ordinarily involve planning individual irrigations.

Instead, the calculations usually estimate ET for the next week or two, and then plan the hours of operation that will be needed during that period to meet crop requirements.

Estimating necessary hours of operation for drip emitters and microsprinklers

The discussion below assumes that you know the ET rate of the crop you are growing, in inches per day. Then follow the three steps below:

Step 1. Convert ET rates to gallons per day.

Use Table 10, below, or do a simple calculation with the following formula:

Water use (gallons/day) $=$ Crop spacing (ft^2) $\times$ ET (in/day) $\times$ 0.623

Example: ET rate is 0.35 inch per day, tree crop spacing 20 feet $\times$ 20 feet $=$ 400 square feet.

Water use $=$ $400 \times 0.35 \times 0.623$ $=$ 87.2 gallons per day

Step 2. Determine the application rate of the irrigation system in gallons per hour.

Use the following formula:

Number of emission devices $\times$ discharge rate per emission device (gal/hr/emitter) $=$ application rate (gal/hr)

Table 10. Converting ET Rates to Gallons per Day

		Evapotranspiration (inches per day)							
		0.05	0.1	0.15	0.2	0.25	0.3	0.35	0.4
Crop Spacing (ft²) = row spacing × plant spacing	100	3	6	9	12	16	19	22	25
	200	6	12	19	25	31	37	44	50
	400	12	25	37	50	62	75	87	100
	600	19	37	56	75	93	112	131	150
	800	25	50	75	100	125	150	174	199
	1000	31	62	93	125	156	187	218	249
	1200	37	75	112	150	187	224	262	299
	1400	44	87	131	174	218	262	305	349
	1600	50	100	150	199	249	299	349	399
	1800	56	112	168	224	280	336	392	449
	2000	62	125	187	249	311	374	436	498
	2200	69	137	206	274	343	411	480	548
	2400	75	150	224	299	374	449	523	598

From Larry Schwankl, Blaine Hanson, and Terry Prichard, *Low-Volume Irrigation*. University of California, Davis, 1993.

Example: Four drip emitters per tree with discharge rate of 0.75 gallon per hour = 3 gallons per hour per tree.

Step 3. Determine the required system operation time in hours per day.

Use the following formula:

$$\frac{\text{ET (gal/day)}}{\text{Net application rate (gal/hr)}} = \text{Hours of operation per day}$$

Example: ET is 62 gallons per day, drip emitters apply 4 gallons per hour, system efficiency 90%. Net application rate is 4 × 0.9 or 3.6 gallons per hour.

62 gallons per day ÷ 3.6 gallons per hour = 17.2 hours per day

Hours of operation for drip tapes and tubings

Follow the two steps below:

Step 1. Use Table 11, next page, to determine the application rate of the drip tape or tubing in inches per hour.

Step 2. Determine needed operation time in hours per day.

$$\frac{\text{Plant water use (in/day)}}{\text{Net application rate (in/hr)}} = \text{Hours of operation per day}$$

Example: ET is 0.3 inch per day, drip tape applies 0.1 inch per hour, system efficiency 90%. Net application rate is $0.01 \times .9$ or 0.09 inch per hour.

0.3 inches per day ÷ 0.09 inches per hour = 3.3 hours per day

Table 11. Application Rate of Drip Tapes and Tubings (Inches per Hour)

Row Spacing (inches)	Flow Rate (gallons per minute per 100 ft.)								
	0.1	0.15	0.2	0.25	0.3	0.35	0.4	0.45	0.5
12	0.1	0.14	0.19	0.24	0.29	0.34	0.39	0.43	0.48
14	0.08	0.12	0.17	0.21	0.25	0.29	0.33	0.37	0.41
16	0.07	0.11	0.14	0.18	0.22	0.25	0.29	0.32	0.36
18	0.06	0.10	0.13	0.16	0.19	0.22	0.26	0.29	0.32
20	0.06	0.09	0.12	0.14	0.17	0.20	0.23	0.26	0.29
22	0.05	0.08	0.11	0.13	0.16	0.18	0.21	0.24	0.26
24	0.05	0.07	0.10	0.12	0.14	0.17	0.19	0.22	0.24
26	0.04	0.07	0.09	0.11	0.13	0.16	0.18	0.20	0.22
28	0.04	0.06	0.08	0.10	0.12	0.14	0.17	0.19	0.21
30	0.04	0.06	0.08	0.10	0.12	0.13	0.15	0.17	0.19
32	0.04	0.05	0.07	0.09	0.11	0.13	0.14	0.16	0.18
34	0.03	0.05	0.07	0.08	0.10	0.12	0.14	0.15	0.17
36	0.03	0.05	0.06	0.08	0.10	0.11	0.13	0.14	0.16
38	0.03	0.05	0.06	0.08	0.09	0.11	0.12	0.14	0.15
40	0.03	0.04	0.06	0.07	0.09	0.10	0.12	0.13	0.14
42	0.03	0.04	0.06	0.07	0.08	0.10	0.11	0.12	0.14
44	0.03	0.04	0.05	0.07	0.08	0.09	0.11	0.12	0.13
46	0.03	0.04	0.05	0.06	0.08	0.09	0.10	0.11	0.13
48	0.02	0.04	0.05	0.06	0.07	0.08	0.10	0.11	0.12
50	0.02	0.03	0.05	0.06	0.07	0.08	0.09	0.10	0.12
52	0.02	0.03	0.04	0.06	0.07	0.08	0.09	0.10	0.11
54	0.02	0.03	0.04	0.05	0.06	0.07	0.09	0.10	0.11
56	0.02	0.03	0.04	0.05	0.06	0.07	0.08	0.09	0.10
58	0.02	0.03	0.04	0.05	0.06	0.07	0.08	0.09	0.10
60	0.02	0.03	0.04	0.05	0.06	0.07	0.08	0.09	0.10

From Larry Schwankl, Blaine Hanson, and Terry Prichard, *Low-Volume Irrigation*. University of California, Davis, 1993.

Water Quality and Salinity

This chapter explains:

• several water quality concerns for irrigators
• salinity concerns for irrigators
• management suggestions for addressing these concerns

Water Quality Problems Caused by Irrigation

Irrigation runoff moving over the soil surface often carries sediments, nutrients (especially nitrogen and phosphorus), salts, pesticides, pathogens, and other contaminants. Even when this water returns to streams, it may be of poor quality: harmful to other irrigators, municipal water users, fish, and wildlife. Deep percolation can also carry these contaminants into local groundwater.

Ground and surface water depletion is a growing concern as competition for water increases among agricultural, urban, and industrial users. Among many other problems, groundwater depletion can cause wells to go dry and can cause salinity and pollution problems in aquifers. Surface water depletion can damage rivers and streams, changing water temperature, concentrating water pollution, and damaging or eliminating fish habitat.

Some strategies for reducing irrigation-related water quality problems include the following:

• Practice good irrigation management, following techniques like the ones described in this book to avoid overwatering and erosion.
• Adjust application rates so they do not exceed the soil's intake rate.
• Adjust furrow flows, reduce furrow grades, or use polyacrylamide (PAM) to prevent erosion.

81

- Follow a nutrient management plan to reduce fertilizer usage.
- Follow an integrated pest management plan to reduce pesticide usage.
- Use conservation tillage to maintain crop residue on the soil surface.
- Install vegetative filter strips to filter out sediments and chemicals.
- Build up the soil's organic matter to increase water-holding capacity.
- Minimize traffic and other factors that can cause compaction.

Poor Quality Irrigation Water

Leach water, tailwater, and runoff from animal agriculture operations, septic systems, and urban areas can all contaminate water bodies used by irrigators. Water contaminated with human pathogens (such as fecal coliform) is a particular concern when applied to crops commonly eaten uncooked. Irrigators should have their water quality analyzed regularly to check for these contaminants.

Poor quality irrigation water is also a major cause of salt-affected soils: those with a high concentration of salts such as the negative ions chloride, nitrate, and sulfate and the positive ions calcium and sodium. Salt buildup often begins with water dissolving salts from fertilizers, manure decomposition, or the weathering of soil minerals. Under humid climate conditions, rain water moves some of these salts into the subsoil while others are taken up as plant nutrients. Under arid conditions, high temperatures and winds evaporate water from the soil surface. Capillary forces draw water upward through the soil, and plants also take up water through their roots, leaving behind dissolved salts.

Sodic soils have a high concentration of sodium. Soil particles saturated with sodium ions repel one another, breaking down the chemical forces that hold soil particles together as aggregates. The result is an impermeable soil structure with poor tilth.

Salt accumulation in the root zone can decrease yields by interfering with the ability of plants to take up water. Under these conditions, plants wilt even though soil moisture levels are high. Plants differ in their sensitivity to salts. For example, at the same level of salinity, beans exhibit a 50 percent reduction in yields while yields of wheat, barley, and sugar beets are unaffected. Seedlings are particularly affected by saline conditions.

Besides hampering the ability of plants to take up water, certain ions are also toxic to plants. Sodium, chloride, and boron, essential nutrients at low concentrations, can be toxic to plants at higher concentrations. If applied through sprinkler systems, salts can produce leaf burn or white spots on foliage—a particular concern for leafy vegetables and floral plants. Water high in sodium ions can corrode metal irrigation lines. Water high in carbonates can clog nozzles.

Addressing the Causes of Salt-Affected Soils

Addressing salinity and sodicity problems requires first identifying the cause of the problem. If you suspect that your irrigation water is causing a salt problem, have your water analyzed for electrical conductivity and specific ions. High electrical conductivity indicates a high concentration of salts.

If a high water table is moving salts upwards into the root zone, you may be able to install soil drainage that lowers the water table. You can also sometimes lower the water table by planting a deep-rooted crop, such as alfalfa.

If high temperatures are evaporating salt-laden irrigation water from a bare soil surface, you may be able to address the problem by mulching or leaving crop residues on the soil surface to reduce evaporation.

In many cases, you can apply water in excess of that needed by plants in order to leach excess salts downward through the soil profile. For this process to work, the soil must have good internal drainage, meaning that it is not compacted, does not have a high water table, and does not have a restrictive rock layer. You may need to repeat this process on a regular basis. The percentage of irrigation water that drains below the root zone is known as the *leaching fraction*. Charts and tables are available allowing you to calculate the leaching fraction needed to keep salinity within acceptable levels for your crop.

❗Caution: Leached drainage water can cause environmental problems downstream. Besides high concentrations of salts, it may also contain pesticide residues, plant pathogens, and human pathogens from manure applications.

Other techniques:

• Keep soils wetter than required for non-saline conditions. This will reduce competition between plant roots and salts for available water.

• Plant crops that are less sensitive to saline conditions. You may also be able to grow plants that will take up and accumulate toxic ions such as chloride and boron.

• Plant seeds on the edges of raised beds to reduce their exposure to saline conditions. Salts tend to accumulate in the center of raised beds.

• For sodic soils, broadcast and incorporate a soluble source of calcium such as gypsum (calcium sulfate) into the soil. Then apply excess irrigation water, activating a chemical reaction that replaces sodium with calcium and leaches the exchanged sodium into the subsoil.

www.ingramcontent.com/pod-product-compliance
Lightning Source LLC
Chambersburg PA
CBHW050124280326
41933CB00010B/1234

Publication Staff

Project Leader . . . . Mike Morris

Writers. . . . . Mike Morris
Vicki Lynne
Nancy Matheson
Barbara Bellows

Layout and Illustrations . . . . Timothy Rice

Acknowledgments

Many advisors and reviewers helped the staff at NCAT create this book. We would like to thank them all:

USDA Natural Resources Conservation staff: Ann Baldwin, John Busch, Arturo Carvajal, Lynn Cornia, David Fischer, Allen Gehring, Stephen Henry, John Hester, Dan Johnson, Carolyn Jones, Rob Krause, Brady McElroy, David Nelson, Leigh Nelson, Merlin Nelson, Clare Prestwich, Stephen Rogers, Bruce Sandoval, Marty Soffran, David Spengler, Alan Stahl, Mark Twyeffort, Dave White, Darol Wilson, Jesse Wilson

Other reviewers and advisors: David Amman, Jim Bauder, David Bausch, Georgia Brensdal, Linzy Browning, Joel Cahoon, Tim Grove, Mike Hansen, Kristin Keith, Ron Lee, Mark Lere, Doug Mawhinney, Mike McLane, Troy Peters, Matt St. Germaine, Dave Scott, Max Stevenson, Brian Wright

Montana Department of Natural Resources & Conservation staff (who created the original 1989 *Montana Irrigator's Pocket Guide):* Greg Ames, Jim Beck, Greg Clouse, John Dalton, John Doubek, Joe Hamm, Jim Headlee, Larry Hoffman, Patricia Kelley, Larry King, Barbara Lien, Vicki Lynne, Daniel Vichorek, Gerald Westesen

NCAT

Since 1976, the private, non-profit **National Center for Appropriate Technology (NCAT)** has been promoting appropriate technologies that enable people to protect natural resources and live better lives. With programs in sustainable energy and sustainable agriculture, and offices in Montana, California, Arkansas, Pennsylvania, Mississippi, and Texas, NCAT offers research, technical assistance, publications, newsletters, conferences, and websites. Visit www.ncat.org.

Funded through the USDA Rural Business-Cooperative Service, NCAT's **ATTRA Program** offers no-cost assistance to farmers and other agriculture professionals. Technical specialists are available to answer your questions about sustainable agricultural production, processing, and marketing, as well as energy efficiency and renewable energy.

Call Monday through Friday:

800-346-9140 (English) 7 A.M. to 7 P.M. Central Time
800-411-3222 (Español) 8 A.M. to 5 P.M. Pacific Time

Or visit www.attra.ncat.org.

NCAT is committed to providing equal opportunities and access to all of its programs and activities, including recruitment and hiring. NCAT prohibits discrimination on the basis of color, race, religion, sex, national origin, age, disability, sexual preference, marital, or veteran status.

Table of Contents

Figures

Handy Conversions and Formulas

Equipment Maintenance

Introduction

This book is a take-to-the-field reference to help irrigators save water, soil, energy, and money, while protecting water quality. The *Equipment Maintenance* half of this book gives specific instructions for keeping your irrigation system running properly. In the pages that follow you'll find:

- Descriptions and diagrams of recommended pumping plant installations.

- Checklists for pumping plant maintenance tasks. Each system component is treated separately, and maintenance tasks are broken down by how frequently they need to be done.

- A pumping plant troubleshooting guide.

- Checklists for distribution system maintenance.

- Suggestions for improving the energy efficiency of your system.

Ｊ The wrench symbol indicates maintenance tasks.

The information here focuses on do-it-yourself tasks and is not intended to be a complete guide. For example:

- This is not intended to be a guide to choosing, planning, evaluating, or designing an irrigation system. The discussion generally assumes that an irrigation system is already in place. Consult your local NRCS office or local irrigation equipment dealer for new and replacement systems.

- There is little discussion of maintaining diversion structures or conveyance structures (pipelines or ditches) for getting water to the farm. The main focus is on the pumping plant and the distribution system for applying water to the field.

Recommended Installations

Centrifugal Pumping Plant Installation with Electric Motor

If you have an older system, your pumping plant might look like Figure 1, (*Poor,* on page 3) on the discharge side. It's a false economy to save money up front by installing smaller valves and fittings. You'll only achieve greater friction loss and higher pumping costs. The next time you rebuild your pump, replace the fittings so that your plant will look like Figure 1, *Ideal.*

An ideal installation should also have:

- A discharge concentric expansion instead of an abrupt change in pipe diameter to minimize head loss, turbulence and air pockets.
- A discharge valve the same diameter as the mainline.

Figure 2, pages 4-5, shows what your pumping plant should look like when pumping from a surface source such as a river or canal. The pumping plant should also have:

Suction Side of Pump

- A well designed and screened sump that keeps trash away.
- Suction line joints that are airtight under a vacuum.
- No high spots where air can collect.
- A suction line water velocity of five feet per second (fps) or less. Two to three fps is best.
- A suction entrance at least two pipe bell diameters from sump inlet.
- A suction lift (vertical distance from water surface to pump impeller) less than 15 to 20 feet.
- An eccentric reducer to keep air from becoming trapped in the reducer fitting.
- A vacuum gauge to indicate whether the primer is pulling a vacuum or just moving air through the pump.

2

Discharge Side of Pump

- A valve size that is the same diameter as the mainline.

- A non-slam check valve to prevent back spin of the pump when shutting pump off.

- An air relief device when a buried mainline is used.

- A discharge line water velocity of less than seven fps. Five fps is best.

- An energy efficient 1800 rpm motor with a 15% safety factor.

- A simple shade over the motor.

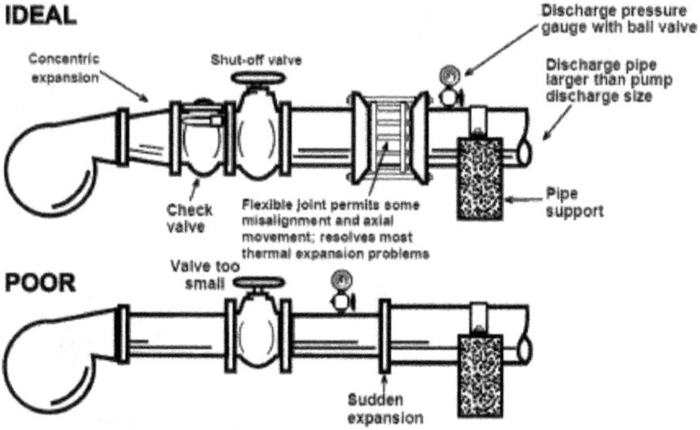

Figure 1. Ideal and Poor Installations (Adapted from *Saving Energy on Montana Farms and Ranches,* Montana Department of Environmental Quality.)

! Caution: Figures 1 and 2 show only components directly related to energy efficiency and do not show pressure relief valves, air vents, or other features necessary for safety and performance. Never let a pump run more than two minutes with the discharge valve closed.

Top View

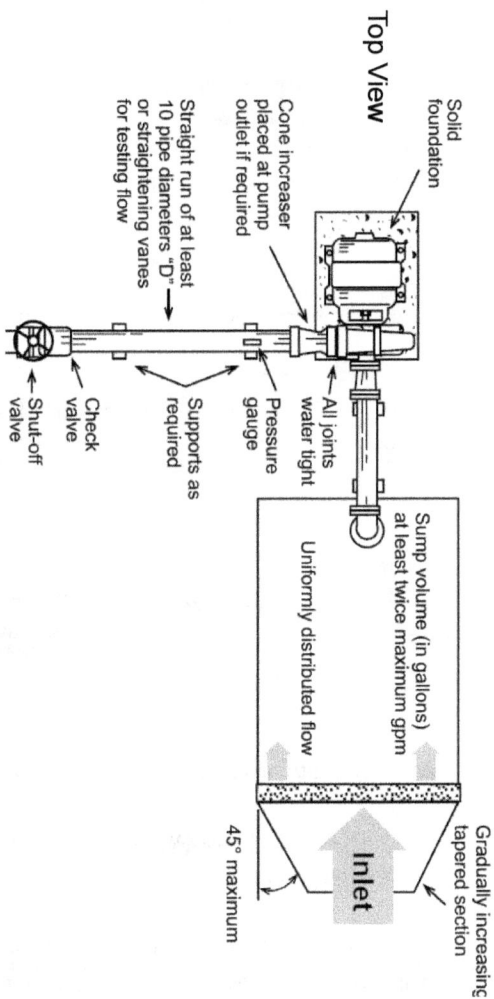

Solid foundation

Cone increaser placed at pump outlet if required

Straight run of at least 10 pipe diameters "D" or straightening vanes for testing flow

All joints water tight

Pressure gauge

Supports as required

Check valve

Shut-off valve

Sump volume (in gallons) at least twice maximum gpm

Uniformly distributed flow

Gradually increasing tapered section

45° maximum

Inlet

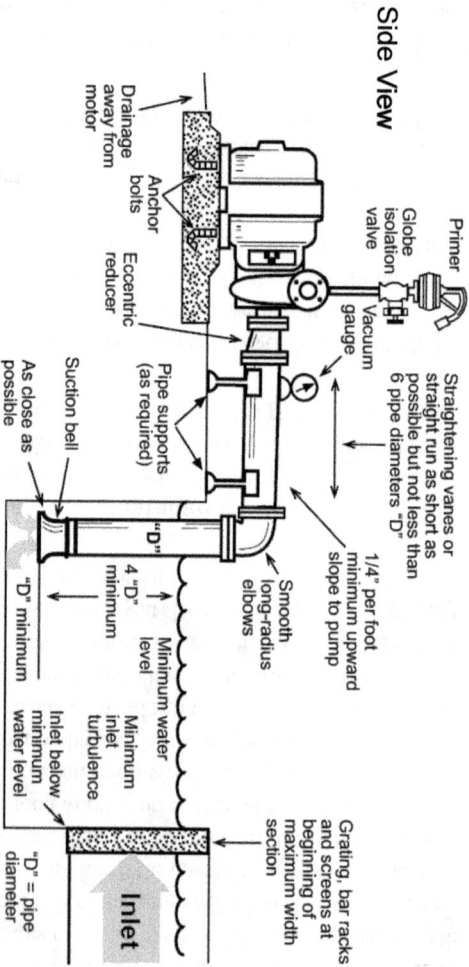

Side View

Primer

Globe
isolation
valve

Vacuum
gauge

Straightening vanes or
straight run as short as
possible but not less than
6 pipe diameters "D"

Anchor
bolts

Drainage
away from
motor

Eccentric
reducer

Pipe supports
(as required)

1/4" per foot
minimum upward
slope to pump

Suction bell

Smooth
long-radius
elbows

As close as
possible

"D"
4 "D"
minimum

"D" minimum

Minimum water
level

Minimum
inlet
turbulence

Inlet below
minimum
water level

Grating, bar racks
and screens at
beginning of
maximum width
section

Inlet

"D" = pipe
diameter

Figure 2. Recommended Pump Installation, Top & Side Views. (Adapted from *Energy Efficient Pumping Standards*, Utah Power & Light Co.)

About Pressure Gauges

A good quality oil- or glycerin-filled pressure gauge on the discharge side of the pump will tell you a lot about your system's condition. If the operational pressure remains close to the original design pressure, the pump is probably in good working order. Pressure changes can indicate clogged suction screens, leaks, pump wear, worn nozzles, and other problems. Use the gauge when filling the mainline to reduce demand and water hammer. Extend the life of your gauge by installing a ball valve on the riser. Keep the valve closed except when referring to the gauge. With a ball valve in place you also have the option of removing the gauge during the winter.

Turbine Pump Installation

Refer to the left half of Figure 3, opposite, for a properly installed turbine pump in a well; many of these same principles apply to turbine pumps in sumps. The properly constructed well should also:

- Be at least six inches in diameter larger than the outside diameter of the well casing when a gravel pack is required.
- Have horizontal well screen slots that continue below the pumping water level. The openings should hold back at least 85 percent of the surrounding material.

The poorly constructed well in the lower right half of Figure 3 shows a well casing that is not centered in the well. Vertical slotted pipe perforations are above the minimum water level, creating cascading water.

Control Panel for Electric Motors

The importance of a properly installed control panel cannot be overemphasized for personal safety and for protecting your investment in your pump and motor.

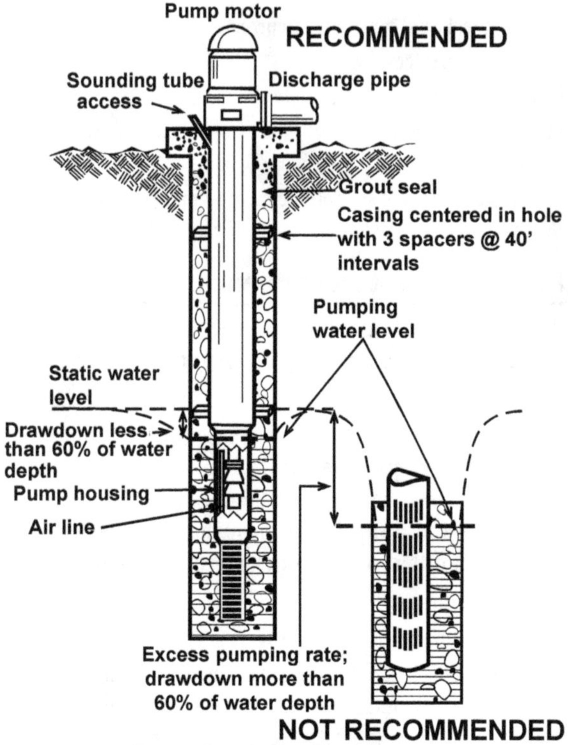

Figure 3. Deep Well Turbine Pump

Your control panel should:

• Have a shade over it to cool thermal breakers.

• Be mounted on secure poles or foundation.

• Have any missing knockout plugs and other holes in the starting switch box replaced and screened or puttied against rodents, insects, and dirt.

• Have a small hole (3/16-inch diameter) in the bottom of the panel to allow moisture to drain.

Your control panel should include the following controls at a minimum:

- Circuit breaker(s) for overload currents
- Lightning arrester
- Surge protector
- Phase failure relay, to protect motor from phase reversal or failure and from low voltage
- A pressure switch to shut off the motor if pumping pressure drops to undesirable levels

Pumping Plant Maintenance

Plan your maintenance and see the benefits in reduced repair costs, lower operating costs, longer system life, and less stress for you.

/ Caution: The recommendations below are not compre-
● hensive and may not be correct for all systems. Consult
your owner's manual for recommended maintenance
procedures and always follow the manufacturer's instruc-
tions if they differ from the ones in this guidebook.

Electric Motors

General

Make a habit of checking to be sure the motor is securely bolted to its platform; mounting bolts can vibrate loose. Also make sure that rotating parts aren't rubbing on stationary parts of the motor, causing damage.

An electric motor is an air-cooled piece of equipment and needs all the ventilation it can get. Excessive heat is the main cause of reduced motor life. Motors also like to be dry. Keep motor windings dry by keeping pump packing in good condition. Even if windings are protected from moisture, minerals in the water can attach to them, causing early failure.

Motors that operate at 3600 rpm experience twice as much wear as motors operating at 1800 rpm. Regular maintenance is especially critical for 3600 rpm motors and pumps.

Maintenance Tasks

At season startup:

- ✓ Remove tape on all openings and clean out rodents, insects, or debris.

- ✓ Locate the motor drain hole on the base or support for the base, and clean it out so water won't be trapped and held directly under the air intake.

- ✓ Change oil in reduced voltage starters using an oil recommended by manufacturer. Be sure to clean the oil pan before refilling.

- ✓ Use vacuum suction or air pressure to remove dust and debris from moving parts of motor. (Don't exceed 50 psi of air pressure.)

Periodically:

- ✓ Clean grass or debris from air ventilation openings on the motor and from around the motor to allow a full flow of cooling air.

- ✓ Check screens on motor ventilation openings. Replace with machine cloth (¼-inch mesh) as necessary.

- ✓ At end of season shutdown cover the motor with a breathable water-resistant tarp.

Motor Electrical System

Winter temperatures can cause electrical connections (especially in aluminum wire) to expand and contract, loosening connectors that were tight in the fall. Loose electrical connections cause heat buildup and arcing at electrical terminals. The voltage drop across loose connections will cause the motor to operate at less than its rated voltage, increasing the internal motor temperature. Increased heat will break down motor winding insulation, resulting in electrical shorts and motor failures. A loose or broken connection can also unbalance the phases of three-phase power and damage the motor windings.

Caution: Before conducting these tasks, be sure power is off at the utility disconnect switch. It may be necessary to have the utility company shut the power off.

Maintenance Tasks

At season startup:

✓ Inspect insulation of motor windings. If the windings are excessively grease-covered, consult your motor repair shop for direction.

✓ Check all safety switches according to manufacturer's directions.

Twice a year:

✓ Check electrical connections from meter loop to motor for corrosion and clean if necessary. Coat the wiring (especially aluminum) and connectors with an antioxidant that meets electrical code requirements.

✓ Check electrical connections from meter loop to motor for tightness. Tighten and re-tape if necessary.

✓ Replace overheated connections or wires with new material. Overheated connections will show heat damage such as burnt insulation on wires.

Motor Bearings

Lubricate the motor according to manufacturer's instructions. Intervals between lubrication will vary with motor speed, power draw, load, ambient temperatures, exposure to moisture, and seasonal or continuous operation. Electric motors should not be greased daily. Bearings can be ruined by either over- or under-greasing.

Fill a grease gun with electric motor bearing grease and label it so it won't be confused with other types of lubricating grease.

Caution: Follow lubrication instructions in owner's manuals if they differ from the ones given here. Newer motors may have sealed bearings that cannot be lubricated.

Recommended Re-greasing Periods for Motors

Type of Service	Horsepower Range		
	1 - 9	10 - 40	50 - 150
Normal Duty (8-hour day)	8 months	6 months	4 months
Heavy Duty (24-hour day)	4 months	3 months	2 months

Maintenance Tasks

✓ Change the grease at recommended intervals to remove any accumulated moisture:

- Remove the bottom relief plug and clean hardened grease out of passage way.
- Using a grease gun, fill housing with approved high temperature electric motor bearing grease (refer to the manufacturer's manual for API number of grease) until old grease is expelled.
- Run motor until all surplus grease is thrown out through the bottom grease port (may require 5 to 10 minutes).
- Shut off motor and use a screwdriver or similar device to remove a small amount of grease from the grease port to allow for grease expansion during full load operation.
- Replace grease plug.

Caution: *Do not overgrease your motor.* **If old grease is not expelled as new grease is pumped in, stop adding grease and have your motor checked by a qualified repair person. Adding new grease without old grease being removed could blow the seals and push grease into the motor. Grease forced into motor windings will cause the motor to overheat and reduce service life.**

Control Panel

Control Panel Safety Precautions

Never use the main disconnect to start or stop your motor. It is not intended for this purpose. Using the main disconnect to start and stop the motor will cause excessive wear of the contacts and arcing can occur. Use the start and stop button.

If the overhead lines to your control panel's service are obstructed by tree branches or other items have the utility company clear the lines.

Have an electrician inspect your panel to ensure that:

- Control circuits are protected with the correct size and type of fuse.
- Lightning arresters are properly installed on the meter and motor side of buss and breaker. They should also be mounted in a secure box to protect you if they blow up.
- The service panel is properly grounded, independently of the pumping plant.
- Service head grommets are in place and in good condition.

General

Have your electrician or pump maintenance person do a Megger check on the control panel, motor, conduits, and other electrical connections. The Megger device applies a small amount of voltage to an electrical component and measures the electrical resistance. A Megger test can also detect potentially harmful moisture in windings.

Any time the main disconnect switch has been left open or off, operate it several times before leaving it closed or on. Copper oxide can form in a few hours and result in poor contact and overheating. Any type of corrosion can cause poor contact, poor grounding, and direct or high-resistance shorts.

❗Caution: After opening the control panel but before touching the controls inside, use a voltmeter to BE SURE that the incoming power is disconnected or turned off. If necessary, have your utility disconnect the power. If you have any doubts about the safety of your control panel, walk away and call a qualified electrician. Even a current of 15 milliamps (one milliamp is one one-thousandth of an amp) can cause serious injury or death. Always play it safe!

Maintenance Tasks
At season startup:

- ✓ Replace fuses after checking to see that they aren't blown. Never use oversized fuses.

- ✓ Operate disconnect switch slowly to check for alignment of blades and clips.

- ✓ Open and close the disconnect switch several times to clean oxide from contact points.

- ✓ Clean contacts of dust and dirt. Clean copper contacts with very fine sandpaper or a fine file. Replace badly pitted or burned contacts. Never file silver or silver-plated contacts. Leave contacts clean and dry so dust won't collect.

- ✓ If accessible, check magnetic starter switch contact points.

- ✓ Clean out debris, rodent droppings, and nests and insects. Make sure drain hole is open.

Control Panel Shutdown (End of Season)

Maintenance Tasks

- ✓ Ensure that switches are in the off or open position. Lock the panel in the off position and remove the fuses to prevent accidental startup and vandalism. Removing fuses will also prevent their corrosion.

- ✓ Protect exposed control boxes against moisture and dust with a waterproof tarp.

Engines: Diesel, Gasoline, Liquid Propane Gas (LPG), and Natural Gas

Make a habit of checking to be sure that the engine is securely bolted to its platform; mounting bolts can vibrate loose. Regularly check coolant, oil levels, fuel, and fan belts. If coolant or oil is down, check lines for leakage. On diesel engines, check injectors and fuel lines for leaks.

Engine power is affected by altitude and air temperature. Derate engine power output by 3.5% for every 1,000-foot increase in altitude over 500 feet above sea level. Derate output by 1% for each 10-degree increase in air temperature above 85 degrees F.

Engine Startup (Beginning of Season)

⚡ *Maintenance Tasks*

- ✓ Remove tape on all engine openings and the distributor cap, and tighten belts.
- ✓ Charge batteries and connect them.
- ✓ Open fuel tank shutoff valve.
- ✓ Before starting the engine, override safety switches that protect against low water pressure, loss of oil pressure, and overheating. After engine has reached operating speed, activate the safety switches.
- ✓ Run the engine for 10 minutes, then turn it off and check oil and coolant levels.
- ✓ Check engine and pump for leaks caused by drying gaskets.

Engine Air System

Always replace disposable air filters with new ones. Cleaning will distort the filter and allow more dirt to enter.

⚡ *Maintenance Tasks*

- ✓ At season startup clean and refill the filter bath in oil-bath air cleaners and reassemble air cleaner.
- ✓ Periodically brush blockage off screen if the air induction system is equipped with a pre-screener.

✓ Change the air filter **only** when the service indicator signals that it's time to change it:
  - Turn off engine before changing air filter.
  - Wipe the outside of the cover and housing with a damp cloth and remove the cover.
  - If cover is dented or warped, replace it.
  - Use extreme care when removing the filter to prevent dirt from falling into the intake duct. Use a clean damp cloth to wipe inside of filter housing.
  - Install new air filter.

Engine Electrical System

Maintenance Tasks
At season startup:

✓ Inspect breaker points for wear and replace if needed.

✓ Set the gap or dwell angle and lubricate rotor.

✓ Check timing and adjust if necessary.

✓ Clean all connecting terminals; cover with protectors.

✓ Spray silicone on electrically operated safety switches and ignition system to prevent corrosion.

Twice a year:

✓ In engines that have them, clean and re-gap spark plugs or replace with plugs in the recommended heat range.

✓ Check all terminals and electrical connections for tightness and corrosion, and spray with corrosion inhibitor (NOT grease).

✓ Remove the distributor cap and lubricate governor weights with silicone (NOT oil).

If you have a natural gas engine, note that natural gas has a higher octane value than gasoline. You can increase engine efficiency and reduce fuel consumption by setting the ignition timing to take advantage of the higher octane. Consult the engine manufacturer for recommendations on how to do this.

Engine Oil and Lubrication

Have a sample of engine oil analyzed for contaminants, which signal abnormal wear. Intervals between analyses will depend on the engine and analysis may be cost-effective only for larger engines. Equipment dealers should know where the oil can be analyzed and how often this should be done.

Use only the oil recommended by the manufacturer. Tag each engine with a label identifying the proper oil.

PUMPING PLANT

Maintenance Tasks
Twice a year:

- ✓ If the engine was not protected during shutdown or if the oil has not been changed within the last year, change the crankcase oil and oil filter.

- ✓ Lubricate all engine accessories such as the driveshaft and U-joints.

Engine Fuel and Coolant

Maintenance Tasks

- ✓ Twice a year remove and clean or replace the fuel filter.

- ✓ Periodically check that fuel tank cap and oil filter cap are on tight and that gaskets aren't cracked.

- ✓ Periodically check that the fluid level and degree of coolant protection are adequate. Check that the radiator cap is on tight and that gaskets aren't cracked.

Engine Shutdown (End of Season)

Maintenance Tasks

- ✓ Drain all fuel from the tank and lines and shut off the fuel valve. If LP gas is used, drain vaporizer-regulator. (Drain both fuel and water lines.)

- ✓ Remove spark plugs. Pour a tablespoon of clean motor oil into each spark plug hole. Position spark plug wire away from cylinder opening and rotate crankshaft by hand to lubricate piston and rings. Replace spark plug.

- ✓ Seal the distributor cap with duct tape where the cap joins the distributor housing.
- ✓ Seal all the openings in the engine with duct tape, including air cleaner inlet, exhaust outlet, and crankcase breather tube.
- ✓ If the engine coolant is water, drain and refill the cooling system with water, a rust inhibitor, and antifreeze.
- ✓ Remove tension from belts.
- ✓ Remove and store batteries in a cool but not freezing location. Do not store batteries directly on concrete.
- ✓ If engine is outside, cover it with a water-resistant tarp.

Centrifugal Pumps

Centrifugal Pump Startup (Beginning of Season)

Maintenance Tasks

- ✓ Using new gaskets and pipe-dope, reconnect to the pump any piping removed during shutdown.
- ✓ Re-install the primer and priming valve if they were removed during shutdown.
- ✓ Check that the pump shaft turns freely and is free of foreign objects. Applying power could break the impeller if it's rusted to the case.
- ✓ Check the pump for leaks caused by drying gaskets.
- ✓ Check intake and discharge piping for proper support and make sure pump is securely bolted to platform.
- ✓ Clean the drain hole on the underside of the pump.

General

To avoid water leaks make sure that all gaskets are the correct ones for the coupling or flange. Refer to the sidebar on gaskets on page 37. Eliminate air leaks in your pump's suction line by coating threaded connections with pipe cement or white lead and drawing them tight. Also examine suction line welds for cracks which will allow air leaks.

17

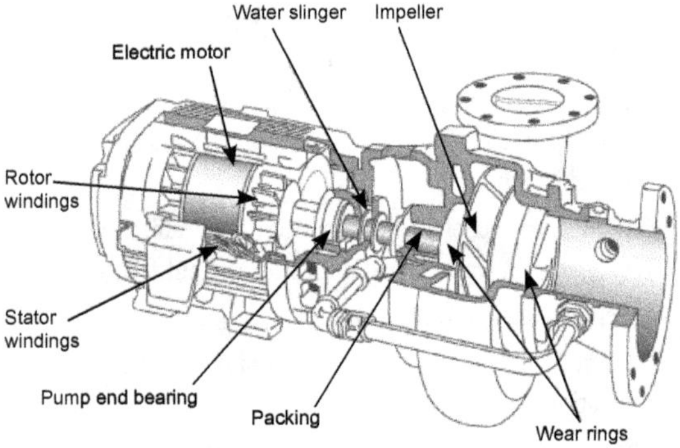

Figure 4. Centrifugal Pump and Electric Motor (Cornell Pump Company, Portland, OR)

If your pump isn't delivering water, verify that the pump shaft is turning in the direction of the arrow on the pump casing. As viewed from the motor end, the rotation is usually clockwise, but check the startup instructions that came with the pump. On three-phase motors, swap any two power leads to change rotation. It is recommended that a qualified electrician perform this task.

If the pump doesn't prime, check for air leaks on discharge valves. Many all-metal gate type valves won't seal properly to create a vacuum. Sand or other debris lodged between the rubber flap and the valve seat will prevent check valves from sealing and forming a tight joint. See if the rubber face is cracked or chipped and not seating. Replace the gate valve or check valve. Check connections between pump and primer. On a hand primer, if grass or other debris is lodged in the check valve, air is pulled back into the pump at every stroke and the pump won't prime. After proper priming, fill the system slowly.

¶ *Maintenance Tasks*
Twice a year:

- ✓ Thoroughly clean suction and discharge piping and connections of moss and debris.
- ✓ Tighten all drain and fill plugs in the pump volute case to avoid air and water leaks. Use a pipe thread compound on all pipe threads.
- ✓ Check for cracks or holes in the pump case.
- ✓ Clean trash screening device and screens on suction pipe.

Servicing Impeller and Wear Rings

If you suspect your pump impeller is clogged with foreign matter, is damaged, or that the wear rings are worn, you can dismantle the pump. This will take some work and is best done in the shop. Or have a qualified pump repair shop undertake this procedure. Follow the directions in the manufacturer's manual, if available, instead of the simplified directions below.

- Remove suction cover or volute case.
- Remove debris from impeller and volute. Remove pebbles lodged between vanes.
- Check wear at impeller eye and vanes. If worn, repair or replace the impeller.
- Re-machine or replace wear ring if clearance is greater than 1/32 inch per side.
- Replace suction cover or volute. Use a new gasket.

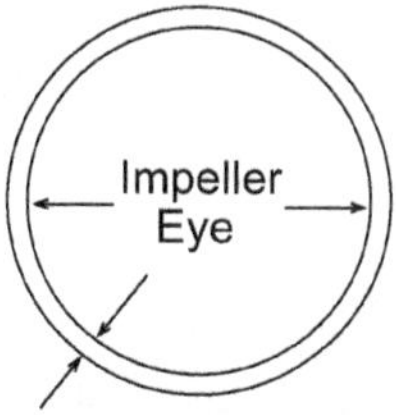

1/32" clearance

Figure 5. Impeller Eye and Wear Ring

19

Net Positive Suction Head (NPSH)
and Cavitation

A centrifugal pump doesn't pull water from a source; it can only pump water that is delivered to it. When air is removed from a suction pipe, as for example by a primer pump, the weight of the earth's atmosphere forces water to rise into the pipe. The maximum height that water can rise in a pipe under a given set of conditions is known as *Net Positive Suction Head* or NPSH.

Under a perfect vacuum and at sea level, atmospheric pressure can theoretically force water to rise as much as 34 feet into a pipe, but this number drops with any increase in elevation, water temperature, or pipe friction. Practically speaking, centrifugal pumps located more than 20 feet above the source water are likely to experience problems.

Insufficient NPSH often occurs when starting irrigation pumps. Since the pump is working against low pressure, it moves a larger-than-normal volume of water, increasing friction losses in the suction line and reducing NPSH. Insufficient NPSH leads to water vaporizing in the eye of the impeller, causing *cavitation*—a noisy condition where vapor bubbles collapse violently in the pump.

If cavitation is allowed to continue, the pump impeller and pump casing can become pitted and damaged. To stop cavitation that is occurring, close the discharge valve. To eliminate pump cavitation and water hammer, and to prevent high amperage draw on demand meters, each time you start up the pump open the discharge valve slowly to fill the mainline.

/ **Caution: Don't let the pump run more than two**
• **minutes with the discharge valve closed.**

Servicing the Pump Packing

A pump with shaft sleeve and packing in good condition and properly adjusted shouldn't require constant re-adjustment, but should be checked daily. If proper leakage (about 8 to 10 drops per minute) isn't running through the packing box, the packing will become overheated and dry out, eventually burning and scoring the shaft sleeve. Excessive dirt, silt, or sand in the water can also score the sleeve.

Check for an improperly greased or worn rotary shaft seal by running the pump and squirting oil on the shaft just outside the seal. Oil drawn into the seal indicates a leak.

If the pump has been out of service, the packing may be dried and hardened. Air can leak into the pump through the packing box and the pump can lose prime.

Maintenance Tasks

✓ Grease the packing box annually with a proper pump packing grease. Less frequent maintenance causes grease to harden, making this task very difficult.

- If packing box is equipped with a grease cup or a grease zerk apply a couple pumps of packing grease to the packing box to force out the remaining water and protect the packing.

- For a packing box without a grease cup or zerk, remove the last two packing rings (see below for replacing packing) and discard. Pack packing grease into the packing box until full. Add two new rings and gently tighten the packing gland slightly to force the grease into the subsequent packing rings. Then loosen the gland.

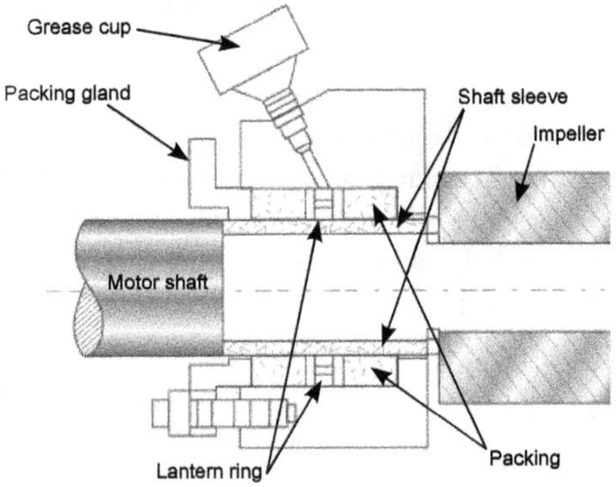

Figure 6. Pump Packing (Cornell Pump Company, Portland, OR)

Replacing the Packing

Old packing should be replaced completely if leakage cannot be reduced by adding a new packing ring to the old packing, or if packing is burned (dried up and scorched) or has leaked excessively during the season. This task is difficult. Have a qualified pump repair shop undertake this procedure. Or if you are attempting the procedure yourself, do it in the shop rather than in the field.

- Remove packing box gland nut with a wrench. Remove gland and packing.
- To remove packing, twist two packing pullers 180 degrees apart into the exposed packing ring. Pull each ring out of the packing box cavity until all are removed. The lantern ring has two holes 180 degrees apart and can be removed with the packing pullers.
- Replace shaft sleeve if worn or grooved; this usually requires pump disassembly. (Once the packing is burned and the shaft sleeve is scored, no amount of adjustment will maintain proper leakage for any length of time.)
- Before replacing new packing, insert the packing gland to make sure it enters freely to the gland's full depth. If it doesn't,

clean out the fragments of old packing and other debris that may be obstructing it.

- Install new packing rings as far forward as can be reached. Install only the type and size of packing recommended by the manufacturer.

- Insert each ring separately. Push it securely into the box and seat it firmly. A small amount of packing grease applied to the packing will make this job a little easier. Don't use sharp points to push the packing into the box. (Use the packing gland, a wooden dowel, pliers handle, fingers, or other blunt object.) Successive rings of packing should be installed so the joints are 120 degrees apart.

- Install lantern ring (if required) in proper position to the packing rings as shown on your manual's parts page.

- Install packing gland so that it just begins to enter the stuffing box straight, so that the full packing is under uniform pressure.

- Seal gland with clip, stud, and nut.

- If the packing is equipped with a grease fitting, add a shot of grease.

- For a packing box without a grease cup or zerk, before inserting the last two packing rings pack grease into the packing box until full. Add the last two rings and tighten the packing gland slightly to force the grease into the subsequent rings of packing. Then loosen the gland.

- Start the pump with the packing gland loose so there will be initial leakage. Tighten the packing gland only enough to draw the necessary vacuum for priming.

- Tighten the gland nuts slightly and evenly every 15 to 20 minutes so leakage is reduced to about 8 to 10 drops per minute or until the water leaking from the box is cool.

! Caution: Don't stop leakage entirely.

Centrifugal Pump Shutdown (End of Season)

It is critical that all water be drained from pumps prior to freezing weather.

Maintenance Tasks

- ✓ Remove suction and discharge piping in areas where ice is a problem. Make sure drain valves are not plugged, and drain water from the pump.

- ✓ Cover any exposed metal, such as the shaft, with protective lubricant to eliminate corrosion.

- ✓ Cover all oil- or grease-lubricated bearings with lubricant so moisture won't rust and pit them.

- ✓ Remove tension from any belts.

- ✓ Open petcock and drain diaphragm-type hand primer.

- ✓ If discharge primer valve is equipped with a rubber seat, coat with rubber preservative.

- ✓ Any rubber parts in a flexible coupling connecting the pump to the driver should also receive a coating of preservative.

- ✓ Make sure ball valve on pressure gauge riser is closed; remove gauge and store inside.

- ✓ Seal all openings, including suction, discharge, and primer, with duct tape against rodents and foreign material.

- ✓ Cover the pump with a waterproof tarp.

Turbine Pumps

General

Some instructions also apply to submersible pumps.

Make a habit of periodically checking that discharge piping is firmly supported in the area near the pump. Make sure pump is securely bolted to platform.

If your turbine pump is installed over a well and you've experienced water supply problems, check the static level and drawdown in the well. A deeper pump setting might be required.

Maintenance Tasks

✓ At season startup, change the oil in the oil bath or reservoir for the pump upper bearings. Fill with approved turbine oil almost to the top of the sight of glass so bearings are covered, taking care that excess oil doesn't get on or in the motor.

Periodically:

✓ Grease lower bearings. Refer to electric motor bearing greasing instructions on page 11.

✓ Maintain the pump packing on water-lubricated turbine pumps as directed on pages 21–23 for centrifugal pump packing.

✓ Annually change the bearing oil in vertical hollow shaft motors. When replacing the oil, follow motor manufacturer's recommendations or use ISO-VG32 turbine oil, such as:

- Mobil DTE 797
- Lubriplate HO-0
- Chevron Turbine Oil GST32
- Shell Turbo T Oil 32

Maintain the bearing oil at the proper level. Overfilling the oil reservoir can cause oil to overflow when the motor heats up during operation. The excess oil will adhere to the motor and to ventilation screens, collecting dirt and debris and reducing the motor's ability to dispel heat.

Short-Coupled Turbine Pump

Maintenance Tasks

✓ At season startup for oil-lubricated pumps, fill the oil reservoir and start the oil flowing to the pump one hour before starting the pump. Check to see that the oil tube is filled before running the pump. The pump needs about 10 drops per minute.

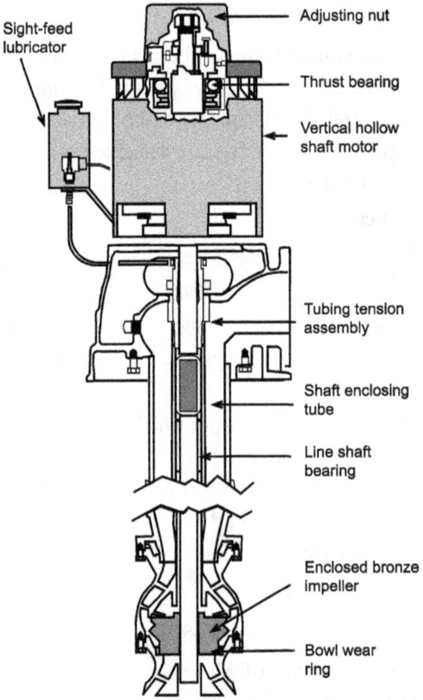

Figure 7. Oil-Lubricated Turbine Pump

✓ At season startup for water-lubricated turbine pumps, pre-lubricate line shaft bearings with light oil.

✓ Periodically adjust and maintain packing on water-lubricated, short-coupled turbines as directed for the packing on a centrifugal pump (see pages 21–23).

✓ Annually (or according to manufacturer's recommended interval) adjust the head shaft nut on short-coupled turbine pumps:

  • Remove top motor cover and take out the set screw.

  • Remove, clean, oil, and replace the key stock.

- Loosen the head shaft adjusting nut (it has a left-hand thread) so the shaft and bowls are resting on the bottom. Tighten the head shaft adjusting nut two turns, which will raise the shaft and bowl assembly enough to allow for proper clearance.
- You should be able to turn the shaft by hand once it's raised. If you can't, tighten the head shaft adjusting nut one-half turn and try to turn it by hand again.
- Replace the set screw and motor cover.

! **Caution: If you are unable to turn the shaft by hand, and you have raised the shaft by five or more turns of the nut, remove the pump and disassemble and inspect for damage or debris. If you have any questions about this procedure, consult your pump dealer.**

Deep Well Turbine Pump

Shaft adjustment needs to be more precise for deep well turbines. Shaft stretch needs to be considered. Refer to the manufacturer's instructions or consult a qualified pump dealer.

Maintenance Tasks

✓ At season startup for oil-lubricated pumps, start lubricating the shaft up to a week before starting the pump, or until the line shaft and column are full of oil and the oil begins to run out at the top near the stretch assembly. During this first week, allow 4 to 5 drops of oil per minute. After starting, increase to 10 to 15 drops of oil per minute. Check the manufacturer's instructions to be sure of the requirement. (Oil will drip slower at night when it cools down.) The viscosity rating of the oil should be 9 or 10.

✓ Periodically adjust and maintain packing on water-lubricated deep well turbines the same as the packing on a centrifugal pump (see page 21-23).

27

Submersible Pumps

A submersible pump is a turbine pump that is close-coupled to a submersible electric motor. Since both pump and motor are suspended in the water, the drive shaft and bearings required for a deep well turbine pump are eliminated. The pump is located above the motor and water enters the pump through a screen located between the pump and motor.

Submersible pumps use enclosed impellers. The motors are smaller in diameter and longer than turbine pump motors. Inadequate circulation of water past the motor may cause it to overheat and burn out. The riser pipe must be of sufficient length to keep the bowl assembly and motor completely submerged at all times and the well casing must be large for water to easily flow past the motor. Electrical wiring from the pump to the surface must be watertight with sealed connections.

Troubleshooting

This section identifies symptoms and possible causes under
Suction, System, and Pump. Find the Symptoms and then look
across to the left to see possible causes. Refer to the Maintenance
section for possible remedies. Most often, suction problems are
the cause. Contact your pump repair shop for additional help.

! **This troubleshooting guide is general and does not
cover all the possible system configurations or problems
that might be encountered.**

Symptoms

Cause of Suction Problems	Pump does not deliver water	Pump has insufficient capacity (gpm)	Pump loses prime after starting	Pump has insufficient pressure	Pump requires excessive power	Packing box leaks water excessively	Packing box has short life	Pump vibrates or is noisy	Bearings have short life	Pump overheats and seizes
Pump not primed	•	•								•
Insufficiently submerged suction pipe inlet	•	•	•							
Pump or suction pipe not completely filled with water	•	•	•					•		
Insufficient Net Positive Suction Head (NPSH — See page 20 for explanation)	•	•						•		•
Suction line, strainer, or centrifugal pump balance line plugged		•					•			
Air leaks into suction line		•	•							

29

Symptoms

Cause of Suction Problems, continued

	Pump does not deliver water	Pump has insufficient capacity (gpm)	Pump loses prime after starting	Pump has insufficient pressure	Pump requires excessive power	Packing box leaks water excessively	Packing box has short life	Pump vibrates or is noisy	Bearings have short life	Pump overheats and seizes
Air leaks into pump through packing box		•	•							
Excessive amount of air or gas in the water		•	•	•						
Foot valve too small, insufficiently submerged, or partially clogged				•				•		

Cause of System Problems

	Pump does not deliver water	Pump has insufficient capacity (gpm)	Pump loses prime after starting	Pump has insufficient pressure	Pump requires excessive power	Packing box leaks water excessively	Packing box has short life	Pump vibrates or is noisy	Bearings have short life	Pump overheats and seizes
Speed (rpm) too low	•	•		•						
Parallel operation of pumps unsuitable	•	•		•						•
Total system head higher than pump design head	•	•		•	•					
Wrong direction of pump rotation	•			•	•					
Speed (rpm) too high					•					
Total system head lower than pump design head					•					

Cause of Pump Problems

Cause of Pump Problems	Pump does not deliver water	Pump has insufficient capacity (gpm)	Pump loses prime after starting	Pump has insufficient pressure	Pump requires excessive power	Packing box leaks water excessively	Packing box has short life	Pump vibrates or is noisy	Bearings have short life	Pump overheats and seizes
Rotary shaft seals (packing) leak air	•									
Foreign matter in impeller	•	•		•				•		
Wear rings worn				•	•					
Impeller damaged				•				•		
Defective pump casing gasket permitting internal leakage				•						
Misalignment of pump and driving unit					•	•	•	•	•	•
Bent shaft between pump and motor or engine					•	•	•	•	•	
Rotating part rubbing on stationary part of motor					•			•	•	•
Packing gland too tight resulting in no water flow to lubricate packing and shaft					•		•			
Packing worn, improperly installed, or incorrect for operating conditions						•	•	•		
Cooling water not getting to water-cooled packing boxes							•			
Packing forced into pump interior						•	•			
Shaft or shaft sleeves worn or scored at the packing						•	•			

Symptoms

Cause of Pump Problems, continued

Cause of Pump Problems, continued	Pump does not deliver water	Pump has insufficient capacity (gpm)	Pump loses prime after starting	Pump has insufficient pressure	Pump requires excessive power	Packing box leaks water excessively	Packing box has short life	Pump vibrates or is noisy	Bearings have short life	Pump overheats and seizes
Shaft running off center						•	•	•	•	•
Impeller or rotor (electric motors) out of balance						•	•	•	•	•
Bearings worn							•	•	•	•
Foundation or platform not rigid or mounting is loose								•		
Pipe not supported								•	•	
Under- or over-greasing of bearings or greasing sealed motor bearings									•	•
Condensation of atmospheric moisture in the bearing housing									•	•
Lack of lubrication or improper lubrication									•	•
Scoring or rusting of bearings in turbine pump									•	•
Improper installation of bearing, incorrect assembly of stacked bearings, and use of unmatched bearings as a pair (turbine pump)									•	•
Excessive thrust (seen as shaft movement from mechanical failure or failure of hydraulic balancing device)								•	•	•

Pumping Plant Maintenance Form

Field #____Year____Beginning date_____Ending date _____

Date pump start-up_____ Beginning PSI _____

Midseason PSI _____ Date _____

End of season PSI _____ Date _____

Motor amps _____ Test date _____

Motor amps _____ Test date _____

Pump:	**Motor:**
Installation Date _____	Installation date _____
Dealer _____	Dealer _____
Mfr. _____	Mfr. _____
Model _____	Model _____
Serial no._____	Serial no. _____
Rated head _____	Rated horsepower _____
Rated flow _____	Service factor _____
Repair date _____	Repair date _____
By _____	By _____
Desc. of repair _____	Desc. of repair _____

Date Replaced or Serviced

	System 1	System 2
Gauges	_____	_____
Motor bearings	_____	_____
Pump packing	_____	_____
Oil change	_____	_____
Filters	_____	_____
Hoses	_____	_____
Cooling system	_____	_____
Lube	_____	_____
Adjust turbine bowls	_____	_____
Primer pump	_____	_____
_____	_____	_____
_____	_____	_____
_____	_____	_____

Distribution System Maintenance

Sprinkler Systems

General

Ideally, aluminum mainlines should be raised off the ground with short boards or old tires to allow air circulation and prevent corrosion.

Lay out mainline and hand line pipe as straight as possible to minimize friction loss through couplers. Install air relief valves and vacuum relief as needed on high points of the mainline and air relief at the end of the mainline. Set the mainline pressure relief valve at 10 psi above normal operating pressure, or at the pressure specified to protect piping.

! **Caution: Irrigation pipes are one of the most common of all sources of human contact with power lines. To avoid serious injury or even electrocution, always look up for power lines BEFORE you start work. Treat all overhead power lines as though they were bare and uninsulated. Keep vehicles, equipment, tools, and people at least 10 feet away from power lines. When lifting, cleaning, and storing pipe sections, never raise the end of a pipe higher than your head. Do not stand a pipe on its end, or you could hit a power line.**

Sprinkler Heads

To make sprinkler system maintenance less of a chore:

• Always keep a few extra nozzles and sprinkler heads on hand for quick repairs.

• Use a box-end wrench to remove and replace sprinkler nozzles. Open-end or pipe wrenches will damage nozzles.

• When reinstalling sprinkler heads, wrap the threads with Teflon plumber's tape. Petroleum-based pipe-dope compounds cause early deterioration of rubber washers. Also, do not lubricate sprinkler heads for either storage or operation.

34

• When installing new sprinkler heads, spray a dab of paint on the new heads. Avoid getting over-spray on rubber or moving parts. Spray that same color on your shop wall and note the year. Use a different color for each year. Since sprinkler heads last one to five years, depending on hours of operation, sediment in the water, and other factors, four or five colors are enough.

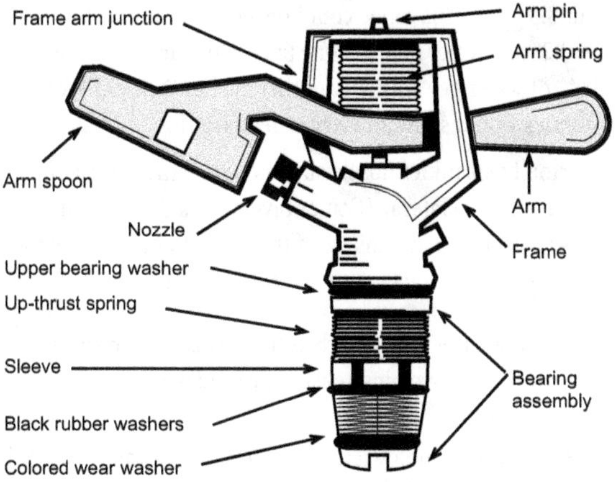

Figure 8. Sprinkler Head (Adapted from *Maintaining Impact Sprinklers*, Oregon State University, Corvallis, OR)

Remember that broken or weak springs cause uneven spray patterns and reduced production due to uneven water distribution.

If your crop land is rolling, with significant elevation changes, consider flow control nozzles. These nozzles will compensate for pressure differences caused by elevation changes. Most models are only effective, however, at pressures between 25 psi and 55 psi.

⸰ Maintenance Tasks
  ✓ Daily check that nozzles aren't plugged. Unplug nozzles with something softer than the material they are made of. *Don't hammer a head to dislodge a plug.*

Over the years, or even within a season, hand lines and wheel lines often acquire a variety of nozzle sizes. This results in a varying amount of water put on your crop. For example, at 50 psi a 9/64″ nozzle puts out 4.1 gpm, an 11/64″ nozzle puts out 6 gpm, and a 13/64″ nozzle puts out 8.5 gpm. This range could result in the application of 0.2″ water per hour on one part of the field and over 0.4″ of water per hour on another part of the field. Worn nozzles would show an even wider variation.

Normally, sprinkler nozzle size should be the same along the length of a lateral. (Center pivots are an exception to this rule.) If you are unsure of the correct nozzle size for your system, contact your local NRCS office.

- ✓ For other problems such as bent arms, broken springs, or broken arm pins, replace the head with one of your extras.
- ✓ At season shutdown remove a few two- or three-year-old sprinkler heads (depending on the amount of silt or minerals in the water, operating time, and other wear-causing variables). If some show wear, remove all sprinkler heads of the same age and check for nozzle wear and worn washers and springs. Replace worn nozzles and heads as needed. See page 58 for the cost of worn nozzles.

Mainlines and Lateral Pipes Startup (Beginning of Season)

Maintenance Tasks
- ✓ Clean pipe of animal nests.
- ✓ Inspect for bent or flattened piping, split seams, and punctures. Use a slightly tapered wooden plug of proper diameter to round out damaged ends.

Choosing Gaskets

Using a gasket in a coupling that it was not made for is a common cause of leaky gaskets. Get the right gasket and the right kind of gasket for the fitting.

Flat gaskets: Most are made of neoprene and are used on flanged, bolt-together fittings. They are usually not expensive. They normally fail by "creeping" out of their fitting. Look for new neoprene gaskets that contain a cotton backing sandwiched in the gasket to reduce the creeping action.

Shaped gaskets: The three most common materials are styrene-butadiene (SBR), ethylene-propylene (EPDM), and polyethylene (poly). SBR and EPDM have much better resistance to cracking, abrasion, ozone, and weathering resistance than poly gaskets. They are more expensive than poly but will last longer. When buying shaped gaskets, look for gaskets that are dull; this indicates that little or no plasticizer has been added to the gasket. Plasticizers significantly reduce gasket life.

- ✓ Reassemble all couplers, gaskets, risers, and sprinkler heads. Replace damaged gaskets. Gaskets shrink and admit air. Tighten flanges or connections, or replace gaskets.
- ✓ If mainline valves leak, replace valve plates or lids.
- ✓ If your mainline valves have grease zerks, lubricate according to manufacturer's instructions.
- ✓ Tap exposed steel pipe with a rubber hammer before startup to release rust.
- ✓ Flush entire system thoroughly with end plugs and wheel line drains removed to prevent plugging nozzles and pressure regulators with any dirt, rust, or other foreign material that may be in system. Replace end plugs and drains.

✓ With water supplied to hand line or wheel line, check all nozzles and impact sprinklers for plugging, mismatched sizes, breakage, corrosion, or other damage caused by wear or winter weather. Check couplers, connections, levelers, and drains for leaks.

Wheel Line Mover and Wheels Startup

If fuel was left in the carburetor through the winter, fuel passages may have become clogged by sediment, residue, or additives.

If gas is not entering the engine cylinder from the carburetor, the carburetor may require adjustment or cleaning before the engine will start and operate properly.

Maintenance Tasks

✓ Remove dirt and debris from mover chain and gears of drive mechanism. Lubricate teeth and chains with SAE 30 weight oil or with grease by wearing rubber gloves and using a bucket full of grease. (Consult the manufacturer or equipment dealer as to which lubricant to use.) Realign drive chains if necessary.

✓ Open hydraulic fluid valve and check hydraulic fluid. Refill if necessary.

✓ Inspect the entire length of the wheel line, checking wheels and power mover for loose bolts, equipment wear, or winter damage. Repair as necessary.

✓ Before starting wheel line mover for the first time in the spring, make sure the drive mechanism is disengaged.

✓ Make sure fuel tank is free of debris and fill with fresh fuel. If fuel tank was not emptied at shutdown or fuel stabilizer was not added, drain it and fill with fresh fuel.

✓ Remove the spark plug. Clean and set the gap. If the spark plug is damaged or shows excessive heat erosion, replace it.

✓ To check operation of power mover, engage transmission and slowly power unit forward or backward to make sure

all wheels, chains, and gears are working properly. Make sure wheel line is straight or the ends are slightly lagging behind the power mover's direction of travel.

Mainlines and Lateral Pipes General (Throughout Season)

Maintenance Tasks
✓ In spring and fall inspect piping for corrosion. If any is found, consult the supplier for protection methods.

Periodically:
✓ Check pipe, valves, drains, and risers for plugging from grass and other debris.
✓ Flush sediment from ends of laterals.

Wheel Line Mover
The cover on the power mover should be closed whenever the mover is not being worked on and especially before turning the irrigation water on. Wheel lines should not be moved with water in the pipeline.

Maintenance Tasks
Throughout the season:
✓ Remove dirt, oil, and debris from the exterior engine surfaces, with special attention to cooling fins, surfaces near air intake, and carburetor linkages.
✓ Lubricate mover teeth and chains with either SAE 30 weight oil or grease.
✓ Check air filter weekly. Clean or replace it after every 25 hours of engine operation. Clean or replace more frequently under extremely dusty or dirty operating conditions. Follow manufacturer's guidelines for cleaning and replacement.
✓ Check engine oil once each week or every five operating hours. Change oil after every 25 hours of engine opera-

39

tion, using a high quality oil. Engine oil should be changed more often if air cleaner shows evidence of extremely dusty or dirty operating conditions. When adding or changing engine oil, do not under- or overfill the crankcase.

✓ Check fluid reservoir of hydraulic transmission every 25 operating hours. Fill to proper level. Drain any water that has seeped into reservoir.

✓ If fluid appears dirty, drain and replace with hydraulic fluid recommended by manufacturer. Replace inline filter in pickup line of transmission.

✓ Grease wheel axles and main drive hub bearings every two weeks with water-resistant multipurpose grease. Follow manufacturer's recommendations for lubrication selection and application.

Mainlines and Lateral Pipes Shutdown (End of Season)

Before shutting down lateral pipe-based systems at season's end, evaluate system components. Look for problems and mark for repair: worn impact sprinklers, nozzles, leaky pipes, gaskets, levelers, and drains. Purchase replacement equipment for installation during spring maintenance activities.

Avoid storing pipe near acids, caustic or other chemical fumes or dusts, and avoid contact with animal waste.

Maintenance Tasks
✓ Flush automatic drains so they are operating and free of sand.

✓ Where freezing is a concern, drain water from all pipelines and completely open valves.

✓ Remove end plugs from wheel lines and empty water, debris, or sediment in pipe ends. Replace plugs.

✓ Dismantle hand lines into sections and store on inclined racks above the ground to permit drainage and air circulation.

- ✓ Remove gaskets, clean off silt, sand, or other debris, and store in a dry place — ideally in a plastic garbage bag and sprinkled with talcum powder to prevent cracking.
- ✓ After the gaskets have been removed, clean couplers with water to remove foreign matter.
- ✓ Wire covers onto the ends of wheel line sections to prevent debris and rodents from entering pipe during the winter. (Three pound coffee cans work well.)
- ✓ If livestock will be in the field, move wheel line to the end of the field and surround with electric fence.
- ✓ To prevent wind damage to wheel lines, secure wheel line to posts driven at every third or fourth wheel.

Wheel Line and Mover Shutdown (End of Season)

If the engine is to be removed at season's end, engine maintenance can be completed after removal.

✂ Maintenance Tasks

- ✓ Start engine and let run for a few minutes. Shut off fuel tank switch and let the carburetor run out of fuel. Drain or siphon out all remaining fuel in the tank and flush out any debris. If you want to leave fuel in the tank, add fuel stabilizer.
- ✓ Remove spark plug and pour a tablespoon of clean motor oil into spark plug hole. Position spark plug wire away from cylinder opening and rotate crankshaft by hand to lubricate piston and the rings. Replace spark plug.
- ✓ Remove mover chain and store in a bucket of used motor oil for the winter.
- ✓ Secure engine cover by latching or tying it in place to keep wind from blowing it open.
- ✓ Avoid placing wheels in a ditch where expansion and contraction of piping can twist the wheels.

Center Pivot & Linear Move Startup
(Beginning of Season)

Most newer pivots and linear move systems operate at low pressure and include pressure or flow regulation devices that are susceptible to plugging. Even small amounts of nozzle fouling will result in a noticeable reduction in water application uniformity. Center pivot and linear move water supply must be clean.

Maintenance Tasks

- ✓ Clean pipe of animal nests.
- ✓ Disconnect electrical power and check that mover motor lead connections are tight and not burned or corroded.
- ✓ Make sure that all equipment is properly grounded.
- ✓ Check and lubricate all valves according to manufacturer's instructions.
- ✓ Grease the center pivot swivel with one full tube of grease.
- ✓ Grease the driveline if equipped with grease-type U-joints, and check for excessive wear.
- ✓ Grease all zerks liberally at least annually.
- ✓ Check tower boxes for damage and seal to keep water out if they show signs of moisture.
- ✓ Check for proper tire inflation. Uneven tire pressure is hard on gear boxes. Fill tires (22-25 psi for 11.9-inch tires, 16-18 psi for 14.9-inch tires) and tighten lug nuts.
- ✓ Flush system thoroughly with drains removed to prevent plugging nozzles and pressure regulators. Replace drains.

Center Pivot & Linear Move General
(Throughout Season)

Maintenance Tasks

- ✓ Annually: Check gear box lubricant to ensure that it's filled to the proper level. Change oil in gearboxes at least every three years. If you operate your pivot or linear move system

more than 1,000 hours a year, change oil every other year. Consult the manufacturer's recommendations for oil type, weight, and service schedule specific to your equipment.

Regularly:

✓ Inspect pipe for corrosion. If corrosion is found, consult the supplier for protection methods.

✓ Check pressure regulators at each sprinkler head. If water leaks out the side air hole during operation, replace it.

✓ Check all nozzles for wear and to ensure that they are spraying properly.

✓ Check that drains are free and working properly.

Center Pivot & Linear Move Shutdown Preparation (End of Season)

Maintenance Tasks

✓ Park the pivot for the winter on level ground if possible, or slightly uphill from pivot center.

✓ Flush automatic drains so they operate free of sand.

✓ Where freezing is a concern, drain water from all pipelines and completely open valves.

✓ Where freezing is a concern, remove drain plugs from gear boxes to let water out that has seeped in. Then replenish with oil. Fill to ¼ inch above the uppermost bearing, or to within ¼ inch of the top if it has an expansion chamber.

✓ Booster pumps may have a mechanical seal in the packing box. If the seal wears out, replace it. Follow shutdown procedures for pumps and motors under Pumping Plant Maintenance.

✓ If possible raise tires and place boards under them, perpendicular to the line of travel, to allow movement as the system contracts and expands over winter.

✓ Disconnect power to the center pivot or linear move system.

Surface Systems: Ditches, Siphon Tubes, & Gated Pipe

⚕ *Maintenance Tasks*

✓ In the spring clean ditches of mud and weeds.

✓ For gated pipe, replace broken gates and clean gaskets.

At season shutdown:

✓ Where freezing is a concern, clear ditches and repair cracks in concrete liners to prevent damage.

✓ Store siphon tubes and system controllers under cover.

✓ Store gated pipe with gasket end facing north to lessen damage from sunlight, and with gates closed and turned up to discourage rodents from gnawing the seals.

Microirrigation Systems

Water quality is critical to maintaining microirrigation systems. Emitter clogging is the greatest problem you face.

⚕ *Maintenance Tasks*
Regularly:

✓ Check for leaks daily or weekly. These are generally easy to spot in surface systems. In subsurface systems, watch flowmeters and pressure gauges closely. *Leaks cause increased flow rate and decreased pressure.*

✓ Inspect filters. Clean and replace as necessary. Backflush filters manually or with automatic cycle. In media filters, replace filter media (such as sand) when it begins to cake.

✓ Install pressure upstream and downstream from filters. A dirty filter increases pressure differential. Follow manufacturer's recommendations for acceptable pressure drop.

✓ Flush lines about every two weeks. If it takes more than about a minute to flush the lines clean, you may need to flush more often.

✓ Inspect emitters for clogging daily or weekly. Completely clogged drip emitters should be cleaned or replaced,

although most are sealed and can't be taken apart for cleaning. Check flowmeters and pressure gauges as an indication of partial clogging. *Clogging causes decreased flow downstream from clogs and increased pressure upstream.*

✓ Check application rate (inches per hour) once or twice per year. For surface systems, catch flow from several emitters in a rain gauge for exactly one minute. For subsurface systems, take pressure measurements and us conversion tables provided by the manufacturer. Sudden changes indicate partly clogged emitters, leaks, or other problems.

✓ Chlorinate system monthly with 10-20 ppm if you have moderate clogging due to biological contamination.

✓ For drip emitters that are completely clogged with biological contaminants, try injecting 50-100 ppm of chlorine. Wait 24 hours and then thoroughly flush the system.

! **Caution: Organic growers are not allowed to have residual chlorine levels exceeding the maximum residual disinfectant limit under Safe Drinking Water Act limit, currently equivalent to 4.0 ppm. Allowed alternatives to chlorine include hydrogen peroxide, alcohols, and soap-based algicide/demisters.**

✓ Clogging due to mineral desposits (such as lime or iron precipitates), can be prevented, and often remediated, by injecting acid to lower pH to 6 to 6.5 every 2-4 weeks. (Measure with pH strips or a pool/spa test kit.)

✓ For emitters that are completely clogged with mineral deposite, try injecting enough acid to lower pH to 5.0. Wait 24 hours and then thoroughly flush the system.

! **Caution: Acid can damage emitters and other irrigation components, with the greatest risk below pH 5.5. The flexible orifice in some pressure-compensating emitters is especially susceptible to acid damage.**

Caution: Organic growers are generally not allowed to use synthetic acids. Many organic growers use vinegar, which contains acetic acid if it is from a natural source.

Caution: Be careful when mixing chemicals. Wear eye protection and gloves and follow instructions. Any carelessness on your part could cause an explosion of caustic chemicals, a release of toxic gases, or a chemical reaction that will severely clog emitters.

Caution: Your system must include appropriate valves, drains, and controls to prevent backflow, which could cause chemicals to contaminate your water source or spill onto the ground.

Caution: Do not mix chlorine and acids (or acidifed fertilizer) together, or store them in the same room, since they will form chlorine gas which is toxic and can cause eye and skin burns, lung damage, and even death.

At season shutdown:

✓ Treat entire system with 40 ppm residual chlorine concentration for at least four hours, and completely flush the system. (Organic growers: see above notes.)

✓ Drain water from all pipelines. The system may have to be blown out lateral by lateral with an air compressor. Don't exceed 15 to 20 psi of air pressure, or you'll blow off the emitters. Polyethylene pipes can withstand some freezing without breaking, so it isn't critical that all water be removed. In cases where remaining water may be a problem, add a gallon of non-toxic antifreeze (the type used in RV's) to the piping system and distribute it throughout with compressed air. More antifreeze may be necessary for larger systems.

Caution: Organic growers are prohibited from using synthetic substances such as RV antifreeze.

Sprinkler System Maintenance Form

Field no.____ Year____ Beginning date_____ Ending date_____

System: _____

Installation date _____ Dealer _____

Mfr. _____ Model _____

Repair date_____ Repaired by_____

Description of repair _____

_____

System: _____

Installation date _____ Dealer _____

Mfr. _____ Model _____

Repair date _____ Repaired by _____

Description of repair _____

_____

Date Replaced or Serviced

	System 1	System 2
Nozzles	_____	_____
Heads	_____	_____
Levelers	_____	_____
Gaskets	_____	_____
Drains	_____	_____
Mainline valve plates/lids	_____	_____
Pressure regulators	_____	_____
Wheel line mover	_____	_____
Engine oil	_____	_____
Hydraulic fluid	_____	_____
Filters	_____	_____
Lube system	_____	_____
Hoses	_____	_____
Pivot drives	_____	_____
End gun booster pump	_____	_____
_____	_____	_____
_____	_____	_____
_____	_____	_____

DISTRIBUTION SYSTEM

Saving Energy

You don't have control over rising electricity costs or low commodity prices, but you can stop throwing money away on inefficiencies in your irrigation system. Start by making regular maintenance a priority. Read the tips here on how to make cost-effective improvements to your irrigation system. Then study the Water Management half of this guidebook to learn how to use your efficiently pumped water most effectively. The results might just amaze you and improve your bottom line.

Electrical Use and the Charges on Your Power Bill

Electricity is measured in watts or kilowatts (equal to 1,000 watts). The number of watts is the product of operating voltage times the current (or amps) flowing to the load. A kilowatt-hour (kWh) is an amount of energy equivalent to using one kilowatt (kW) over a one-hour period. To visualize one kilowatt-hour, it may be helpful to imagine ten 100-Watt lightbulbs burning for one hour.

Although billing procedures vary among electric providers and in different regions of the country, irrigation bills typically include three basic charges for electricity:

1. The Base Rate or Meter Charge. This is either a monthly or seasonal charge. Some utilities roll this charge into the electric consumption or energy rate.

2. Electric Consumption or Energy Charge. This charge is based on the amount of electricity used over time as recorded on the kilowatt-hour meter, with a rate charged for each kWh consumed.

3. Electric Demand Charge. Many utilities charge their larger customers an amount over and above the charge for kilowatt-hour energy consumption, in order to maintain enough capacity to serve these large customers' needs. Electric pro-

viders generally calculate the demand charge in one of two ways, each method intended to give an approximation of the customer's size:

a. The demand charge may be based on connected load or horsepower, with a fixed rate charged per horsepower during each billing period. This charge is usually based on "nameplate" horsepower. For example, if your demand charge is $10 per horsepower your demand charge for a 40 horsepower system would be $400.

b. The demand charge may be based on maximum wattage during the billing period. In this method a special demand meter might measure a wattage for each 15-minute interval during the billing period – almost 3000 intervals each month. (Strictly speaking, the demand meter measures wattage every few seconds and then averages these measurements at the end of the 15-minute interval to calculate an average wattage for the interval.) The demand charge is based on the 15-minute interval during the billing period with highest wattage.

For example, suppose your demand charge is $10 per kilowatt and your demand meter records wattage of 29 kilowatts for some 15-minute intervals in the billing

Time-of-Use Rate Schedules

In some parts of the country, irrigators can sign up for a time-of-use billing schedule. Under time-of-use billing, rates are higher at peak times (when demand is greatest) and lower at "off peak" times. Time-of-use billing allows some irrigators to adjust their work schedules so they irrigate when rates are low, reducing costs and avoiding power interruptions. If time-of-use billing is available in your area, call your utility to discuss this option and see if a time-of-use rate schedule may work for you.

period, 30 kilowatts for other 15-minute intervals, and 31 kilowatts for other intervals. You would be billed $310. A key point is that demand charges are based on the size of your system – not how many hours you operate the system. You would incur a demand charge even if you operated your irrigation system for just one 15-minute interval during the entire monthly billing period. Customers with small motors may not have a demand charge.

Every kWh Counts

Some irrigators mistakenly assume that since they are charged for demand, they won't save money by turning off their pumps and reducing hours of operation. It's true that the demand charge is often a substantial percentage of your total electric bill. But all electric providers bill for every single kWh that is consumed by the irrigation system. You will always save energy and money by reducing your hours of operation.

You can save money by understanding how and when you are charged for electricity. Talk to a customer service representative at your utility for an explanation of the rate structure. Make sure you know when your meter reading date is each month, since this can influence your management decisions. If your power bill includes a demand charge, remember that this charge will be about the same whether you operate your system for one day or 31 days during a billing period.

Common Causes of Wasted Energy

Some common causes of inefficiency and wasted energy are listed below. While some system troubles require expensive repairs, most can be corrected with minor adjustments that have a short payback period.

Causes of High Demand

Your demand meter can alert you to potential problems with your irrigation system. Track your demand amount (kW) over the season and compare the months. Also compare these readings to your demand readings from previous years.

• Is the demand increasing gradually even though you haven't made changes to your system? This might indicate leaks that are growing in volume, increasing pump wear, or increasing wear in motor bearings.

• Did the demand take a sudden jump from one month to the next? This might signal a sudden large leak or significant problem in your pumping plant.

• Is your average demand too high for the connected horsepower? The demand reading on your power bill in kW should be about ¾ of your connected horsepower. (For example, a 40 horsepower pump should have a demand reading of about 30 kW if no other loads are on this meter. If a pivot mover or booster pump are on this meter, the kW will be ¾ of the whole connected load.)

Significantly higher demand may indicate motor overloading, inadequate bearing lubrication, voltage imbalance, or other problems. Consult your irrigation equipment supplier for assistance in determining possible causes.

Lack of system maintenance:

✓ Develop a regular maintenance schedule. Impellers that are out of adjustment, plugged screens, worn nozzles, engine drive units that need a tune-up, worn shaft sleeves, leaking gaskets and drains, and dried out bearings and pump packing are only a few of the problems that you can avoid with regular maintenance.

ENERGY

51

The wrong pump for the system:

✓ If your pump is oversized, undersized, or just not the right one for your system, it will never be able to operate efficiently. While it may be possible to trim the pump impeller, re-nozzle the sprinklers, or redesign the layout of the mainline and laterals, a new pump with different characteristics is most likely necessary.

Pump wear from cavitation or abrasion:

✓ Cavitation damages pump impellers, reducing efficiency. If your pump is cavitating, determine whether you have sufficient NPSH. Refer to page 20 for an explanation of NPSH. You should also have a valve on the discharge side of your pump to allow filling the mainline slowly, avoiding cavitation.

✓ If your water source contains a high amount of sediment, re-engineer your intake structure to allow sediment to settle out of the water before entering the suction line.

Improperly sized or designed fittings:

✓ Every minute that water is passing through undersized fittings, such as valves, at a high velocity, your profits are draining away. Replace those fittings with ones of the correct size. Refer to pages 2-8 for the right way to do it.

Water source changes:

✓ If you're using a well for irrigation and the water table has dropped, you may have to reset the pump at a lower level. To compensate for the increased head, you may have to add more stages to turbine or submersible pumps. If you're using surface water and the level has dropped, centrifugal pumps may have to be relocated closer to the water source in order to supply sufficient NPSH.

✓ If turbine or submersible pump capacities do not fit the well characteristics, you may need to replace the bowls with new bowls suited to your well capacity.

Hardware Improvements

Some common efficiency improvements are listed below. No matter what kind of system you are operating, you'll probably find at least one cost-effective idea below for improving your irrigation system.

Electric Motors

✓ Rebuild your older motor and gain several percentage points in motor efficiency. This procedure typically involves replacing the bearings, rewinding, and "dipping and baking," and is done by qualified motor repair shops.

✓ Consider a premium efficiency motor instead of a standard efficiency motor in all new installations, if the cost of rewinding exceeds 65% of the price of a new motor, and when replacing over- or undersized motors. Premium efficiency motors are 2% to 4% more efficient than standard efficiency motors. Besides saving energy, premium efficiency motors usually have higher service factors, longer insulation and bearing lives, and less vibration than standard efficiency motors.

! Caution: Some premium efficiency motors draw a higher startup current. Make sure your system can handle it.

✓ If you are putting in a new system, be aware that an 1800 rpm motor is more efficient than a 3600 rpm motor. For example: an open drip-proof 3600 rpm, 40-hp motor is 91.7% efficient whereas an 1800 rpm, 40-hp motor is 93% efficient. Since an 1800 rpm motor makes half the revolutions of a 3600 rpm motor, maintenance needs are lower and motor life is longer.

✓ Consider a variable speed drive (also called a variable frequency drive) if you need a pumping plant to produce a wide range of flows and pressures to meet varying system needs. For example, a pump that serves three pivots runs at the same speed whether one, two, or three pivots are op-

erating. A pump with a variable speed drive would run at a slower speed with one pivot turned on, a higher speed with two pivots operating, and at full speed with all three pivots in operation. How cost-effective a variable speed drive is depends on operating hours, pump size, and crop value.

✓ Constant-pressure valves or flow-control nozzles may be as effective as a variable speed drive. Contact your equipment supplier for more information.

Engines

✓ Keep your engine drive in peak operating condition to reduce fuel costs and downtime. Refer to the section on Maintenance for tune-up help.

✓ If your radiator-cooled engine uses a cooling fan, the engine efficiency is reduced by 5-8%. In other words, 5-8% of the fuel going into the engine is used to run the fan, not pump water. You can install equipment that uses the irrigation water to cool the engine, eliminating the need for a fan. Check with an engine equipment dealer for more information.

✓ Think about using the variable speed ability of the engine driving the pump to your advantage. By varying the rpm of the engine you can vary the flow rate, the total dynamic head, and the brake horsepower requirements of the pump to meet varying system needs and save fuel. Consult an engine equipment or irrigation equipment dealer for advice.

Centrifugal Pumps

✓ Rebuilding your older pump to increase its efficiency can be a cost-effective alternative to purchasing a new pump. Rebuilding usually involves replacing shaft sleeves, packing, wear rings, and re-machining or replacing the impeller.

✓ For optimum efficiency, the pump must match the requirements of the water source, the water delivery system, and the irrigation equipment. If your pump is under- or oversized and does not match the system needs, pump replacement is the best option. Running an oversized pump with a mainline valve half-closed is like driving your car with your foot on the brake and the accelerator at the same time.

Turbine Pumps

✓ Vertical shaft turbine pumps will lose efficiency if they are not regularly adjusted. Refer to the Maintenance section for a description of how to adjust a short-coupled turbine pump. Qualified pump service personnel should adjust deep well turbine pumps.

✓ Rebuilding your older turbine pump to increase its efficiency is usually a cost-effective alternative to purchasing a new pump. Rebuilding usually involves replacing shaft sleeves, packing, bearings, and re-machining or replacing the bowls.

Mainlines

✓ Mainlines too small for the volume of water pumped through them contribute to high head requirements and lowered system efficiency. Water velocity through a mainline should never exceed seven feet per second (fps). Velocities below five fps are best, and are achievable through good design. Refer to the Conversions and Formulas section for recommended maximum flow rates for different pipe sizes. Your local irrigation equipment dealer or NRCS office can offer technical assistance to determine if your system's mainline is the right size.

Sprinkler Systems

✓ You can realize significant energy and demand savings by converting a high-pressure pivot with impact sprinklers to low pressure (20 to 35 pounds per square inch or psi)

or very low pressure (10 psi) and installing drop tubes. Reduce your pump size or have the impellers trimmed to reduce horsepower. In addition to saving energy and money, you'll increase water application uniformity because wind drift will be reduced and the water discharge point will be closer to the crop and ground. Be aware that a low pressure pivot could exceed your soil's infiltration rate, causing runoff.

✓ Sprinkler options have come a long way in the last decade. Spinners produce larger droplets that are more rain-like and reduce wind drift. Dual sprayheads allow for different spray options for crop germination or irrigating later in the season. Spray plates can be replaced to allow for different spray patterns. Check out sprinkler packages at your local irrigation equipment dealer to find one suitable for your operation.

✓ You can also convert your pivot to Low Energy Precision Application (called LEPA) by installing hoses or drag socks on the drop tubes. The water is applied directly at the soil surface, virtually eliminating wind drift. These systems also eliminate deep wheel tracks because the ground is wet behind the wheels not in front of them. This type of pivot conversion will not work for all crops (for example, tall ones like field corn) or situations.

✓ Eliminate your pump completely or reduce your horsepower requirements and pump size by taking advantage of gravity if you have sufficient elevation drop. Two and three-tenths (2.3) foot elevation drop is equal to one psi of pressure. Your local irrigation equipment dealer or NRCS office may be able to help you determine if your system can be converted to a full or partial gravity system.

✓ Producers raising orchard and intensive vegetable crops can benefit by converting from hand-move laterals or other high pressure sprinklers to drip or micro sprinklers.

How Leaks Cost You Money

Mainline and distribution leaks and missing sprinkler heads are common to all sprinkler systems. Many producers aren't very concerned about leaks in the field because the water is ending up on the field anyway. What they don't realize is that leaks reduce system pressure, causing a poor sprinkler distribution pattern. Reduced pressure also moves the pump operating point from where it is most efficient and increases demand costs. Significant leaks can also cause motor overload and shorten motor life.

These operate on very low pressure and allow precise placement of water to a limited area of soil adjacent to the plant (which also reduces weed problems.)

Sprinkler Nozzle Wear

To check nozzle wear, remove the nozzle and clean out the interior. Then:

• Use a numbered drill index with bits measured in thousandths or use a new high speed drill bit. If a drill bit is used, get a new nozzle to compare alongside the worn nozzle.

• Insert the index into the nozzle opening and compare the size to that printed on the nozzle.

• Or, insert the shank (smooth end) of the drill bit into the nozzle opening. The fit should be snug. If you can wobble the bit sideways even slightly, the nozzle is worn.

Surface Irrigation

✓ Many surface irrigators can save water and energy by replacing open ditches with *gated pipe*. Gated pipe allows water to flow out through evenly-spaced "gates" or openings along the length of the pipe, giving irrigators increased control over the way water is applied.

ENERGY

57

✓ If you're already using gated pipe, increase the water application efficiency and reduce runoff by installing a surge valve. Surge flow automatically alternates the water from one set of furrows or border strips to another, smoothing the soil and causing the water stream to advance much faster. Deep percolation at the upper end is reduced and water penetration at the lower end is increased for more even water distribution. Depending on crop value and labor costs, a system often pays for itself in a few years.

How Worn Nozzles Cost You Money

Just a tiny bit of nozzle wear (a few thousandths of an inch) can cause a big increase in sprinkler output and can seriously decrease the system's application efficiency. Worn nozzles, like leaks, are one of the most common and underrated problems with irrigation systems and a primary cause of increased electrical demand costs. They also decrease pumping plant efficiency and overload motors, leading to substantially reduced motor life. Depending on your system's total dynamic head and efficiency and your electric costs, *each* worn sprinkler nozzle might be costing you anywhere from $0.25 to $5.00 or more annually.

Handy
Conversions & Formulas

Flow Rate Conversions

Gallons Per Minute (gpm)	Cubic Meters Per Hour	Acre Feet Per 24 Hours	Cubic Feet Per Second (cfs)	Acre Inches Per 24 Hours
1	0.2270	0.004	0.00223	0.05
4.403	1			
224.4		1	0.50	11.9
448.8	101.9	2	1	23.8
673.2		3	1.50	35.7
897.6		4	2.00	47.6
1,000.0		4.5	2.23	54.0
1,122.0		5	2.50	59.5
1,346.4		6	3.00	71.4
1,570.8		7	3.50	83.3
1,795.2		8	4.00	95.2
2,244.0		10	5.00	119.0
2,692.8		12	6.00	142.8
3,141.6		14	7.00	166.6
3,590.4		16	8.00	190.4
4,039.2		18	9.00	214.2
4,488.0		20	10.00	238.0

Miner's Inches

1 ft³/sec	= 50 Miner's inches in ID, KS, ND, NE, NM, SD, UT, WA, Southern CA
1 ft³/sec	= 40 Miner's inches in AZ, MT, OR, NV, Northern CA
1 ft³/sec	= 38.4 Miner's inches in CO

One cubic foot per second (cfs) is equivalent to a volume of water 1-foot wide, 1-foot long, and 1-foot high passing a given point every second.

One acre inch is a volume that would cover one acre of land one inch deep. One acre foot would cover one acre one foot deep.

One acre inch per 24-hour day requires 18.7 gpm continuous flow.

A flow of one cfs for one hour = 0.99 acre-inch.

A continuous flow of 1 gpm per acre = 0.053 inches per 24-hour day.

$$\text{gpm} = \text{cfs} \times 448.8 \qquad \text{cfs} = \text{gpm} \times 0.00223$$

$$\frac{\text{Gross application of water}}{\text{(in acre inches per acre)}} = \frac{\text{gpm} \times \text{hours}}{450 \times \text{number of acres}}$$

Volume Conversions

Liters	Gallons	Cubic Feet	Cubic Meters	Acre Inches	Acre Feet
1	0.2642	0.0353			
3.785	1	0.1337	0.003785		
28.32	7.48	1	0.02832		
1000	264.2	35.314	1		
	27,154	3,630		1	0.0833
	325,850	43,560	1233.5	12	1
	1 million				3.07

Weight Conversions

1 kilogram	= 2.20 pounds	= 1,000 grams
1 gram	= 28.4 ounces	
1 pound	= 7,000 grains	
1 gallon of water	= 8.33 pounds	
1 cubic foot of water	= 62.4 pounds	

60

CONVERSIONS & FORMULAS

Length Conversions

Inches	Links	Feet	Yards	Meters	Rods/Poles	Chains	Kilometers	Miles
7.92	1							
12		1		0.3048				
36		3	1	0.9144				
39.37		3.28		1			0.001	0.000622
	25	16.5	5.5		1			
	100	66	22		4	1		
		1093.61	1000				1	0.62137
		5280	1760	1609	320	80	1.61	1

Area Conversions & Formulas

Square Meters	Acres	Hectares	Square Feet	Square Yards	Square Rods	Square Chains
1	0.000247	.0001	10.76	1.196		
4049	1	0.405	43,560	4,840	160	10
10,000	2.471	1	107,639	11,960		

Number of square feet × 0.000023 = acres
Number of square yards × 0.00021 = acres
Number of square rods × 0.0062 = acres
Number of square chains × 0.10 = acres

Area of triangle = ½ base × height

Area of rectangle = length × width

Area of circle = $\pi \times radius^2$ **or** $3.1416 \times radius^2$

Circumference of circle = $\pi \times diameter$ **or** $3.1416 \times diameter$

Temperature Conversions

$$°F = (1.8 \times °C) + 32$$

$$°C = \frac{(°F - 32)}{1.8}$$

Power Conversions

Kilowatt	Horsepower	BTU/hour
1	1.341	3,413
0.746	1	2,545

Electrical Formulas

Single Phase Power Supply

Electric Demand $= kW = \dfrac{V \times I}{1000}$

Electric Consumption or Energy $=$

$kWh = kW \times hours = \dfrac{V \times I \times hours}{1000}$

Where: $V = voltage \quad I = current\,(amps) \quad kW = kilowatts$

Three Phase Power Supply

Electric Demand $= kW = \dfrac{V \times I \times 1.73}{1000}$

Electric Consumption or Energy $= kWh = kW \times hours$

$= \dfrac{V \times I \times 1.73 \times hours}{1000}$

Kilowatt (kW) $=$ Electric Demand $= 1000$ watts

Kilowatt-hours (kWh) $=$ Electric Consumption
$= 1000$ watts $\times$ hours $= kW \times$ hours

To find approximate annual operating hours for an irrigation system, divide average monthly demand from your electric bills by total kWh over the whole irrigation season (found by adding together the kWh numbers in your power bills).

Example: Your average monthly demand was 25 kW and you used a total of 27,650 kWh during the irrigation season. 27,650 kWh ÷ 25 kW = 1106 operating hours.

Pressure Conversions

Pounds per Square Foot	Inches of Head	Kilo-Pascals	Feet of Head	Inches of Mercury	Pounds per Square Inch	Atmospheres
1	0.1926	0.0479	0.01605	0.01414	0.00695	0.000473
5.1972	1	0.249	0.08333	0.07343	0.0361	0.002454
20.886	4.022	1	0.331	0.296	0.143	0.0099
62.32	12	3.024	1	0.88	0.4335	0.0295
70.7262	13.6185	3.3864	1.1349	1	0.491	0.033421
144	27.73	6.985	2.31	2.03	1	0.068
2,116.22	407.5	101.32	33.93	29.92	14.7	1

Estimated Pressure Loss; pounds per square inch (psi) lost per 100 feet of pipe

gpm	3/4-inch pipe			1-inch pipe			1.5-inch pipe			2-inch pipe			3-inch pipe		
	S	PE	P	S	PE	P	S	PE	P	S	A	P	S	A	P
2	0.83	0.45	0.39												
5	4.55	2.43	2.14	0.26	0.14	0.12	0.17	0.09	0.08	0.05	0.06	0.02			
10		8.79	7.74	1.40	0.75	0.66	0.63	0.34	0.30	0.19	0.20	0.09	0.03	0.03	
15				5.07	2.72	2.39	1.34	0.72	0.63	0.40	0.43	0.19	0.06	0.05	0.03
20					5.75	5.06	2.28	1.22	1.07	0.68	0.72	0.32	0.10	0.09	0.05
30						8.63	4.83	2.58	2.27	1.43	1.54	0.67	0.21	0.19	0.10
40							8.22	4.40	3.87	2.44	2.62	1.15	0.36	0.33	0.17
50								6.65	5.86	3.68	3.96	1.74	0.54	0.50	0.25
60									8.21	5.16	5.54	2.43	0.76	0.70	0.36
70										6.87	7.38	3.24	1.01	0.93	0.47
80												4.15	1.29	1.19	0.61

S = Steel Pipe   PE = Polyethylene Pipe   A = Aluminum Pipe   P = Plastic Pipe

Example: A system with a flow of 20 gpm through 1.5-inch polyethylene pipe is losing 1.22 psi per 100 feet of pipe.

Note: Multiply psi lost × 2.31 to get feet of head lost.

Estimated Pressure Loss: pounds per square inch (psi) lost per 100 feet of pipe, continued

gpm	4-inch pipe			6-inch pipe			8-inch pipe			10-inch pipe			12-inch pipe		
	S	A	P	S	A	P	S	A	P	S	A	P	S	A	P
100	0.54	0.35	0.24	0.07	0.05	0.03									
150	1.30	0.75	0.51	0.16	0.10	0.07	0.04	0.03							
200	1.90	1.58	0.87	0.27	0.18	0.12	0.06	0.04	0.03	0.02					
300	4.10	2.75	1.85	0.57	0.40	0.26	0.14	0.09	0.06	0.05	0.03	0.02			
350		3.60	2.35	0.75	0.50	0.34	0.19	0.12	0.08	0.06	0.04	0.03	0.02		
400		4.65	3.20	1.00	0.65	0.44	0.24	0.16	0.11	0.08	0.05	0.04	0.03	0.02	
450			4.00	1.20	0.80	0.55	0.30	0.19	0.14	0.10	0.06	0.05	0.04	0.03	
500			5.00	1.50	1.00	0.67	0.36	0.24	0.17	0.12	0.08	0.06	0.05	0.04	0.03
600				2.10	1.38	0.95	0.51	0.34	0.23	0.17	0.11	0.08	0.07	0.05	0.03

S = Steel Pipe   A = Aluminum Pipe   P = Plastic Pipe

Estimated Pressure Loss: pounds per square inch (psi) lost per 100 feet of pipe, continued

gpm	4-inch pipe			6-inch pipe			8-inch pipe			10-inch pipe			12-inch pipe		
	S	A	P	S	A	P	S	A	P	S	A	P	S	A	P
700				2.80	1.85	1.25	0.70	0.45	0.31	0.23	0.15	0.10	0.10	0.06	0.04
800				3.60	2.40	1.60	0.87	0.55	0.39	0.29	0.18	0.13	0.12	0.08	0.06
900				4.40	3.00	2.00	1.10	0.72	0.50	0.36	0.24	0.17	0.15	0.10	0.07
1000					3.60	2.45	1.33	0.87	0.61	0.45	0.28	0.21	0.19	0.12	0.08
1200					5.00	3.50	1.90	1.18	0.85	0.63	0.41	0.29	0.26	0.17	0.12
1400						4.55	2.55	1.65	1.12	0.85	0.54	0.38	0.35	0.23	0.16
1600							3.20	2.15	1.42	1.10	0.69	0.48	0.45	0.29	0.20
1800							4.00	2.65	1.79	1.34	0.90	0.60	0.56	0.36	0.25
2000							4.90	3.20	2.20	1.65	1.10	0.74	0.69	0.45	0.30

S = Steel Pipe   A = Aluminum Pipe   P = Plastic Pipe

Example: A system with a flow of 1,400 gpm through eight-inch steel pipe is losing 2.55 psi per 100 feet of pipe.

Adapted from *Montana Irrigation Manual*, USDA Natural Resources Conservation Service, Bozeman, MT.

Water Velocity Formula

Water velocity in feet per second (fps) = 0.409 × flow in gallons per minute divided by the pipe diameter (in inches) squared.

$$= \frac{0.409 \times \text{flow (gpm)}}{\text{pipe diameter (inches)}^2}$$

Example: 300 gpm through a 6-inch diameter pipe

$$= \frac{0.409 \times 300}{6^2} = 3.4 \text{ fps}$$

Recommended Maximum Flow Rate for Different Pipe Sizes

Pipe Diameter (inches)	2	3	4	5	6	8	10	12	16
Flow rate (gpm)		50	110	200	310	440	780	1225	1760	3140

Note: For maximum efficiency, water velocity in the suction line should not exceed 5 fps; 2 to 3 fps is best. Water velocity in the mainline should not exceed 7 fps; less than 5 fps is best. Increasing the pipe size, reducing the flow rate, and changing the pipe type can save energy by lowering the water velocity.

Other Pumping Plant Formulas

Total Dynamic Head (TDH) (feet) =

       Total Lift (Suction & Discharge)

    + Pressure Head

    + Velocity Head

    + Pipe Friction Loss

Discharge Lift (feet) = Distance, in feet, from the centerline of the pump impeller to the pressure gauge.

Suction Lift (feet) = Distance, in feet, from the water level on the suction side of the pump to the centerline of the pump impeller.

Pressure Head (feet) = The pounds per square inch (psi) from a gauge at or near the pump discharge flange × 2.31 (psi × 2.31).

Example: If the gauge reads 20 psi, the Pressure Head
= 20 psi × 2.31 = 46.2 feet

Velocity Head (feet) = The water velocity in feet per second
squared divided by 64.35 $= \dfrac{(\text{fps})^2}{64.35}$

Example: Using the water velocity found on preceding page,

$$= \dfrac{(3.4\,\text{fps})^2}{64.35} = 0.18\,\text{feet}$$

Note: In most irrigation pumping systems, velocity head can be ignored.

Pipe Friction Loss (feet): See the table on pages 64-66. Multiply psi losses time 2.31 to get feet of head loss.

Example: A system with 300 gpm flowing through 6-inch steel pipe is losing 0.57 psi or 1.32 feet of head per 100 feet of pipe. If the system is 200 feet long, Pipe Friction Loss = 2.64 feet.

Water Horsepower (WHP)

$$= \dfrac{\text{System gallons per minute (gpm)} \times \text{TDH (in feet)}}{3{,}960}$$

Input kW (for pumps with electric motors)

$$= \dfrac{3.6 \times \text{Revs} \times \text{Kh} \times \text{PTR} \times \text{CTR}}{\text{Time (seconds)}}$$

Where: *Revs* = *No. of meter revolutions (usually 10)*
        Kh = *Meter Constant (noted on electric meter)*
     PTR = *Transformer Ratio (usually 1)*
     CTR = *Transformer Ratio (usually 1)*
   Time = *No. of seconds it takes for the meter to make 10 revolutions*

Electric Horsepower (EHP) = Input kW × 1.34

Diesel Input Horsepower (IHP$_{\text{diesel}}$)

$$= \dfrac{\text{Gallons of Diesel used per hour}}{55}$$

Propane Input Horsepower ($IHP_{propane}$)

$$= \frac{\text{Gallons of Propane used per hour}}{36.15}$$

Natural Gas Input Horsepower ($IHP_{natural\ gas}$)

$$= \frac{\text{dKt of natural gas used per hour}}{392.9}$$

Note: *1 dKt = decatherm = 1,000,000 Btu. Contact your natural gas supplier for an appropriate conversion to decatherms (dKt), if needed.*

Overall Pumping
Plant Efficiency $= \dfrac{\text{WHP}}{\text{EHP}}$ OR $\dfrac{\text{WHP}}{\text{IHP*}}$

*Diesel, propane or natural gas

Brake Horsepower (BHP)

$= \dfrac{\text{Motor Efficiency} \times \text{EHP}}{100}$ OR $\dfrac{\text{Motor Efficiency} \times \text{IHP}}{100}$

Pump Efficiency $= \dfrac{\text{WHP}}{\text{BHP}}$

Net water application per irrigation period (inches)

$$= \frac{\text{set time (hrs)} \times \text{flow rate (gpm)} \times 96.3 \times \text{system efficiency}}{\text{irrigated area (square feet)}}$$

Set time (hours)

$$= \frac{\text{net water application (inches)} \times \text{irrigated area (sq ft)}}{\text{flow rate (gpm)} \times 96.3 \times \text{system efficiency}}$$

For **surface irrigation systems,** a handy formula is:

Set time (hours) $=$

$$\frac{\text{gross water application (inches)} \times \text{area irrigated (acres)}}{\text{flow rate (cfs)}}$$

A Simple Method to Estimate Your Pumping Plant Efficiency

Pumping plant efficiency measures the amount of power produced by the pump (known as *water horsepower*) per unit of input power (known as *input horsepower*).

When the system is operating under normal, stable conditions, follow the steps below:

Step1. Find total dynamic head (TDH) in feet.

Read pressure from gauge _____ psi × 2.31 = _____ feet

Add height* if pump is **above** water surface   + _____ feet

OR

Subtract height* if pump is **below** water surface   – _____ feet

To get total dynamic head (feet).   _____ TDH

* Height is the distance from the water surface to the centerline of the discharge pipe.

Step 2. Find flow rate in gallons per minute.
If your system has a flow meter, read the gallons per minute (gpm). If the meter reads in cubic feet per second (cfs), multiply times 448.8 to get gpm.   _____ **gpm**

If your system doesn't have a flow meter, you can do a *bucket test*:

2a. Bucket test for hand move, side roll, or linear move systems:

Measure the flow of one sprinkler per lateral that is situated on relatively level ground. The selected sprinkler should be 1/3 down the length of the lateral from the mainline. Use a hose to direct the flow into a five-gallon bucket. Using a stopwatch, estimate the time in seconds to fill the bucket. For greater accuracy, take more than one reading per sprinkler and average the times. Repeat for other sprinklers on other laterals.

Number of seconds to fill bucket   = _____ seconds

Average gpm/sprinkler = 300 divided by the number of seconds

300 ÷ _____ seconds   = _____ gpm

Total flow per hand line or wheel line

= Avg gpm per sprinkler × # of sprinklers   =_____ gpm

2b. Bucket test for pivots:

If you are using a pivot irrigation system and don't have a flow meter:
First, measure the flow of one sprinkler in each set of nozzle diameters along the pivot using the method described in 2a.

Seconds to fill bucket	Average gpm/ sprinkler	No. sprinklers in each set	Total gpm in each set
300 ÷ _____ sec =	_____ gpm ×	_____ =	_____ gpm
300 ÷ _____ sec =	_____ gpm ×	_____ =	_____ gpm
300 ÷ _____ sec =	_____ gpm ×	_____ =	_____ gpm

Total Flow = _____ gpm

Next, estimate flow from end gun using end gun pressure and nozzle diameter from table below.

= _____ gpm

Estimated end gun flow in gpm

Diameter of end gun nozzle (inches)

PSI	½	¾	1	1½	2
10	23.6	53.2	94.4	212	378
20	33.4	75.3	134	300	534
30	40.9	92.2	164	368	654
40	47.2	106	189	425	755
50	52.8	119	211	485	845

Finally, add sprinkler flow to end gun flow to calculate total flow for pivot.

= _____ gpm

Step 3. Find water horsepower (WHP), from Steps 1 and 2.

_____ (TDH) × _____ (gpm) ÷ 3,960 = _____ WHP

Step 4. Find input horsepower (IHP).

4a. For electric motors, locate the meter constant on the electric meter faceplate: marked Kh and followed by a number such as 57.6 or 43.2. Using a stopwatch, time the number of seconds it takes for the disk in the meter to make 10 revolutions, or for the little bar to move across the screen 10 times. If your meter shows kilowatt demand, simply multiply this number times 1.34 to get input horsepower.

48.1 × _____ (Kh) ÷ _____ (secs) = _____ **IHP**

_____ (KW) × 1.34 = _____ **IHP**

4b. For diesel engines, divide gallons of fuel used per hour by 55 to get input horsepower. (Divide gallons per hour by 36.2 for propane. Or divide decatherms of natural gas per hour by 392.9.)

_____ (gallons per hour) ÷ 55 = _____ **IHP**

Step 5. Determine pumping plant efficiency, using results from steps 3 and 4.

_____ (WHP) ÷ _____ (IHP) = _____ % **Efficiency**

Step 6. Compare your efficiency to expected values below.

Rated Motor Size (HP)	Expected Efficiency (%)
3 to 5	66 %
7.5 to 10	68 %
15 to 30	69 %
40 to 60	72 %
75 +	75 %

Note: These efficiencies are for older pumps in excellent condition. New pumps and pumps used under mild conditions or improved design will have higher efficiencies.

Any system whose pumping plant efficiency is less than 65% has some room for improvement. A result in the 50% range or lower indicates a significant problem requiring attention.

Note that improving pumping plant efficiency does not always save energy, unless hours of operation are reduced. Increasing pumping plant efficiency may simply increase flow rates without reducing energy. consumption.